W9-APH-558

The History of Rock and Roll

Stuart A. Kallen

LUCENT BOOKS
A part of Gale, Cengage Learning

GALE
CENGAGE Learning

Detroit • New York • San Francisco • New Haven, Conn • Waterville, Maine • London

LIBRARY OF CONGRESS CATALOGING-IN-PUBLICATION DATA

Kallen, Stuart A., 1955-
    The history of rock and roll / by Stuart A. Kallen.
        p. cm. -- (The music library)
    Discography: p.
    Includes bibliographical references and index.
    ISBN 978-1-4205-0694-5 (hardcover)
    1. Rock music--History and criticism--Juvenile literature. I. Title.
    ML3534.K33 2012
    781.6609--dc23

                          2011031204

Lucent Books
27500 Drake Rd
Farmington Hills MI 48331

ISBN-13: 978-1-4205-0694-5
ISBN-10: 1-4205-0694-3

Printed in the United States of America
1 2 3 4 5 6 7 15 14 13 12 11

CONTENTS

FOREWORD

In the nineteenth century, English novelist Charles Kingsley wrote, "Music speaks straight to our hearts and spirits, to the very core and root of our souls. . . . Music soothes us, stirs us up . . . melts us to tears." As Kingsley stated, music is much more than just a pleasant arrangement of sounds. It is the resonance of emotion, a joyful noise, a human endeavor that can soothe the spirit or excite the soul. Musicians can also imitate the expressive palette of the earth, from the violent fury of a hurricane to the gentle flow of a babbling brook.

The word *music* is derived from the fabled Greek muses, the children of Apollo who ruled the realms of inspiration and imagination. Composers have long called upon the muses for help and insight. Music is not merely the result of emotions and pleasurable sensations, however.

Music is a discipline subject to formal study and analysis. It involves the juxtaposition of creative elements such as rhythm, melody, and harmony with intellectual aspects of composition, theory, and instrumentation. Like painters mixing red, blue, and yellow into thousands of colors, musicians blend these various elements to create classical symphonies, jazz improvisations, country ballads, and rock-and-roll tunes.

Throughout centuries of musical history, individual musical elements have been blended and modified in infinite ways. The resulting sounds may convey a whole range of moods, emotions, reactions, and messages. Music, then, is both an expression and reflection of human experience and emotion.

The foundations of modern musical styles were laid down by the first ancient musicians who used wood, rocks, animal skins—and their own bodies—to re-create the sounds of the natural world in which they lived. With their hands, their feet, and their very breath they ignited the passions of listeners and moved them to their feet. The dancing, in turn, had a mesmerizing and hypnotic effect that allowed people to transcend their worldly concerns. Through music they could achieve a level of shared experience that could not be found in other forms of communication. For this reason, music has always been part of religious endeavors, from ancient Egyptian spiritual ceremonies to modern Christian masses. And it has inspired dance movements from kings and queens spinning the minuet to punk rockers slamming together in a mosh pit.

By examining musical genres ranging from Western classical music to rock and roll, readers will find a new understanding of old music and develop an appreciation for new sounds. Books in Lucent's Music Library focus on the music, the musicians, the instruments, and on music's place in cultural history. The songs and artists examined may be easily found in the CD and sheet music collections of local libraries so that readers may study and enjoy the music covered in the books. Informative sidebars, annotated bibliographies, and complete indexes highlight the text in each volume and provide young readers with many opportunities for further discussion and research.

Three Chords and an Attitude

Rock and roll: The term is understood by people in almost every nation on earth. It describes a type of music—and an attitude—that made history and continues to do so. The music style started out in the United States as a new type of dance music for teenage baby boomers during the mid-1950s. By the 1960s, the music had transformed the cultural—and political—landscape. Never before in history has a style of music come along that so quickly and so completely changed the world.

From the very beginning, rock and roll—and the musicians who performed it—challenged existing social norms, provoking defiance, disrespect for authority, and, at times, revolution among its fans. In the modern world, rock-and-roll music continues to define what it means to be a young person. Rock stars and their songs affect the way people look, dress, act, and talk.

Based on the Blues

Although rock and roll has had complex implications for the entire world, it is some of the simplest music around. Often described as consisting of three chords and an attitude, most rock songs are made up of the basic note patterns that originated in the blues music developed during the nineteenth century. But those ingeniously played three chords can be used behind an infinite number of melodies and woven into the fabric of songs with lead guitars, bass guitars, horns, keyboards, and other instruments. Add a few extra chords and a melody filled with rock-lyric poetry, and the formula for about 95 percent of all rock songs is in place.

Despite the straightforward rock-song recipe, the music is not simplistic. Like the United States, the land of its birth, rock and roll is a melting pot. The music is a synthesis of sounds that includes jazz, country, blues, gospel, and ethnic music from Africa, Latin America, and elsewhere. As more than a sum of its parts, rock music can encompass many different sounds, including the angry, one-chord buzz-saw

Electric guitars like the Gibson Les Paul, played here by Jimmy Page of Led Zeppelin, transformed rock-and-roll music in the 1950s and continue to be a favorite of musicians today.

sound of a punk band, the trippy "sound pictures" of Pink Floyd, the sweet harmonies of *NSYNC, or the eccentric soaring brass and screaming strings of Arcade Fire.

Music Plus Electricity

Rock music embraces so many sounds because it is a child of technology; through the decades, its very sound has been determined by advances in musical and recording equipment. From the earliest days of fifties rock, the music was shaped by the sound of electric guitars like the Gibson Les Paul and Fender Stratocaster, favorites of rock guitar players even today. By 1963 Fender alone was selling fifteen hundred guitars a week. Amateur musicians, who, in another era, might have learned to play the violin or trumpet, were now picking up electric guitars to play rock and roll. By the end of the sixties, anyone who purchased a "fuzz" tone distortion box, a wavelike phase shifter, or a wah-wah pedal could imitate the sounds of rock gods like Jimi Hendrix and Jimmy Page of Led Zeppelin.

Changes in recording technology impacted the sound of rock more than the electric guitar. During the mid-1960s the Beatles worked in the studio for months, inventing sound by manipulating primitive recording equipment to produce a single song with unusual sound effects. A decade later, with the advent of multitrack recording technology, instrumental and vocal performances could be easily layered on top of one another to achieve a cohesive sound with a sonic sweep unmatched in earlier eras. New sounds from synthesizers and drum machines further broadened the rock musical palette.

In more recent decades, the melding of music and computers has added an entirely new dimension to rock and roll. While most rock music had previously been recorded in specialized multimillion-dollar studios, musicians in the first decade of the twenty-first century could crank out hit records on laptop computers using inexpensive digital software like Pro Tools. In 2011 Apple introduced its GarageBand audio recording app for iPad tablet computers. This meant that for less than five dollars, rock musicians could record with power, portability, and sophistication beyond the wildest dreams of the Beatles or Hendrix.

Digital technology has expanded the ways people make, buy, and listen to rock and roll, and the music has invaded nearly every aspect of life. A roomful of long-playing vinyl records from the 1960s now fits onto a cell phone or an MP3 player smaller than a pack of gum. The iTunes store has more than 14 million songs available at the click of a mouse. This means rock music is heard everywhere. It is played in school classrooms and at world-class sporting events such as the Olympics and the Super Bowl. The music propels a multibillion-dollar industry dominated by some of the largest corporations in the world.

Music Is Love

Rocker David Crosby once sang that music is love. He meant that rock and roll has become a universal language among fans, allowing them to enjoy songs together even if they speak different languages. As a source of joy and inspiration, rock and roll has put an indelible stamp upon the world. Although not all of rock's influences have been positive, there is a lot to love in a style of music that has brought so much happiness to so many people in so many places throughout the years.

CHAPTER 1

Good Rockin' Tonight

Rock and roll's most distinctive element is rhythm, and nearly every musical style that helped spawn rock music has a powerful beat that makes people want to dance. The roots of rock rhythm were born centuries ago in African tribal music, with its strong drumbeats that highlight the second and fourth beats, called backbeats, in each four-beat measure. The highlighting of only certain beats in a measure is called syncopation. When a syncopated backbeat is emphasized, the rhythm makes people want to clap their hands, tap their feet, and dance. In a very real sense, syncopation is the heartbeat of rock and roll.

Another aspect of tribal music that found its way into rock and roll was the traditional vocal style known as call and response, in which a song leader sings a line and a group of singers repeats it. This singing technique was brought to American shores by black slaves, who modified it for use in church gospel singing. The call-and-response style was also used in work songs known as field hollers.

By the end of the nineteenth century, African American musicians were using modified call and response, syncopation, and field hollers in a new style of music called the blues. Blues songs incorporated three basic chords with flexible gliding melodies, or blue notes, which lie at the roots of rock.

Singing the Blues

In 1910 blues music was popularized nationwide by William Christopher (W.C.) Handy, a composer and trumpet player who was the son of former slaves in Alabama. Handy wrote the song "Memphis Blues" in 1912. Two years later he composed "St. Louis Blues," the most frequently recorded American song of all time. In his fascinating 1941 autobiography, *Father of the Blues*, Handy described how the blues were born:

> Southern Negroes sang about everything. Trains, steamboats, steam whistles, sledge hammers, fast women, mean bosses, stubborn mules—all became subjects for their songs. They accompanied themselves

W.C. Handy

In 1883, when blues pioneer W.C. Handy was only ten years old, he was able to pick out musical notes in the sounds of nature. In his captivating 1941 autobiography titled Father of the Blues, *Handy explains that these sounds gave birth to the blues:*

Whenever I heard the song of a bird and the answering call of its mate, I could visualize the notes in the scale. Robins carried a warm alto theme. Bobolinks sang contrapuntal [counterpoint] melodies. Mocking birds trilled cadenzas. Altogether, as I fancied, they belonged to the great outdoor choir.

There was a French horn concealed in the breast of the blue jay. The tappings of the woodpecker were to me the reverberations of a snare drum. The bullfrog supplied an effective bass. In the raucous call of the distant crow I would hear the jazz motif. The purple night would awaken a million crickets with their obbligatos [indispensible musical lines] of mournful sound, also the katydids [grasshoppers]. [And] down the lonely road the hooves of the galloping horses beat in syncopation. . . . As I grew older I added the saxophonic wailing of the moo-cows and the clarinets of the moody whippoorwills [nocturnal songbirds]. All built up within my consciousness a natural symphony. This was the primitive prelude to the mature melodies now recognized as the blues.

W.C. Handy. *Father of the Blues*. New York: Macmillan, 1941, p. 14.

on anything from which they *can* extract a musical sound or rhythmic effect, anything from a harmonica to a washboard. In this way, and from these materials, they set the mood for what we now call the blues.[1]

In the early twentieth century blues music was adapted by white Southern musicians, who added their own musical styles to the mix, such as traditional English country ballads. This musical synthesis, popularized by Jimmie "The Singing Brakeman" Rodgers in the late 1920s, gave rise to country or "hillbilly" music. The style was essentially the blues as interpreted by white people in the rural South.

Boogie-Woogie Beat

Jazz was another musical tributary that fed into the flow of rock and roll. This style of music originated at the beginning of the twentieth century in New Orleans, Louisiana, when musicians combined elements of blues, ragtime, Mardi Gras dance music, and European military marches. With so many elements coming together, it was natural that musicians would pick and choose melodies and musical passages from a variety of sources, making up melodies on the spot rather than reading notes from previously written music scores. This led to the musical improvisation that provides the foundation of jazz. Players referred to improvised musical passages as riffs or licks. The style of musical

White Man's Blues

Jimmie Rodgers, one of the most popular "hillbilly" singers in history, was born in a tiny town in the Mississippi Delta in 1897. He worked as a brakeman on railroad trains before he became a best-selling artist on the Victor label in 1927. Larry Starr, a professor of music, and Christopher Waterman, a professor of arts and culture, explain how Rodgers, now known as the father of country music, was influenced by blues music:

> One major reason for Jimmie Rodgers' success was his receptivity to African American influences, complimented by his ability to reflect those influences in original compositions and performances that proved appealing to a substantial white audience. In a highly successful series of recordings called "blue yodels," he adapted the poetic and musical forms of the blues, and aspects of blues performance styles, to his own purposes. The first such record, called simply "Blue Yodel" (also known by its opening words, "T for Texas") was a million-seller . . . informed by Rodgers' distinctive approach to what can only be called "white man's blues."
>
> Rodgers' blue yodeling was a "high lonesome sound" analogous in certain ways to the [wordless] moans and howls heard in blues recordings by rural black artists, and serving much the same purpose: to underline the intensity and depth of the singer's feelings.

Larry Starr and Christopher Waterman. *American Popular Music from Minstrelsy to MTV*. New York: Oxford University Press, 2003, p. 113.

improvisation they pioneered later influenced jam bands like the Grateful Dead and Phish.

In the late 1940s the most innovative jazz bands were smaller combos that featured a guitar, stand-up bass, piano, drums, and a small horn section. These groups took the jazz style, blended it with blues, increased the musical intensity and the tempo, and pioneered a new form of music known as boogie-woogie, or rhythm and blues (R&B).

Boogie-woogie features a strong backbeat, hot improvised solos by individual players, and blues-based lyrics shouted over the music. The "walking" bass line is emphasized and embellished by a stand-up bass player who slaps the strings, giving the music an irresistible beat.

When singer, songwriter, and saxophone player Louis Jordan combined the boogie-woogie style with jazz and blues, he created a hybrid called jump blues. This style of up-tempo, hard-driving dance music helped make Jordan one of the most successful African American musicians of the twentieth century. His string of number-one songs recorded between 1941 and 1952, like "Caldonia," "Choo Choo Ch'Boogie," and "Daddy-O," earned him the nickname "King of the Jukebox."

The Rocking Craze

Louis Jordan's jump blues inspired Wynonie Harris, an African American R&B singer credited as one of the founding fathers of rock and roll. In December 1947, Harris electrified listeners, both black and white, with his recording of "Good Rockin' Tonight." The song features a rollicking boogie-woogie piano, loud hand claps on the backbeat reminiscent of gospel music, and a walking bass line behind Harris's shouted-out vocals.

Most of Harris's late 1940s songs celebrate drinking, partying, and rocking and rolling. A list of his mischievous song titles makes it easy to see why white teenagers of the era thrilled to the forbidden world inhabited by Harris and other early rockers: "Lollipop Mama," "Drinking Wine Spoo-Dee-Oodie," "I Want My Fanny Brown," and "All She Wants To Do Is Rock." Harris faded away during the mid-fifties rock explosion, but like many of his fellow blues shouters, including Roy Brown and Bull Moose Jackson, he ignited a "rocking" craze that paved the way for a generation of white rock and rollers.

"Rock Around the Clock"

One of the first white musicians to take advantage of the rock craze was a Philadelphia, Pennsylvania-based country singer named Bill Haley. In 1951 Haley recorded a countrified version of the swinging song "Rocket 88." Although the record failed to sell, Haley opened his show with the song when he played in local barrooms and at high school proms. The

Alan Freed's Moondog Show

Alan Freed is a seminal figure in the history of rock and roll. He coined the term *rock and roll* and was the first disc jockey to play the style of music for white teenagers. Freed originally hosted a classical music show on WJW radio in Cleveland, Ohio. In 1951 a local record store owner told Freed that hundreds of white teens were buying R&B records by black artists. Freed persuaded WJW to let him spin some of the R&B records after midnight, and his *Moondog Show* was born.

The *Moondog Show* went out on a 50,000-watt clear channel in Cleveland, and the signal was so strong it skipped across the stratosphere to a vast area of the Midwest. Teenagers could tune in from rural towns, big cities, and suburbs to hear Freed spinning records, chattering wildly, and beating on a Cleveland phone book with a drumstick. Freed was so popular that he was signed by WINS, the biggest radio station in New York City in 1954. He hosted Alan Freed's *Rock and Roll Party* until 1957, but was fired when it was revealed he took money from promoters to play certain records on his show.

song went over so well, Haley added another jump blues song to his repertoire called "Rock the Joint." These songs created so much excitement that Haley dumped his country band, with their cowboy outfits, and hired a tight combo of jazz musicians, which he named His Comets. Haley taught the band choreographed steps he had seen performed by black R&B groups, and they found inspiration at their rehearsals playing records by African American jump blues bands.

Haley hardly looked like someone destined for stardom. Dressed in a plaid jacket with a lock of hair falling over his forehead, the stout Haley looked rather like someone's goofy uncle. But it was the sound that mattered, and his song "Crazy Man, Crazy" went to number twelve on the *Billboard* magazine pop charts in 1953.

The growing popularity of Bill Haley & His Comets landed the group a contract with Decca Records, a major record label, and the company released the band's novelty song "Rock Around the Clock" in 1954. The song, which clocks in at a little more than two minutes long, was written by a sixty-three-year-old professional tunesmith named Max Freedman. It was a minor hit for Haley, lasting only one week on the *Billboard* charts after peaking at number twenty-three.

Sheer Volume

"Rock Around the Clock" caught the attention of the producers of a controversial 1955 movie *Blackboard Jungle*, and they decided to use it over the opening credits of the film. *Blackboard Jungle* is about juvenile delinquents who terrorize teachers—and each other—in an inner-city school. When teenage filmgoers heard "Rock Around the Clock," they were up and dancing in the theater aisles within seconds. In some cities the song provoked near riots. Although there is nothing revolutionary in the lyrics, rock critic James Miller describes why the song made such a huge impact:

> Wishing to use the song as a symbol of youthful mayhem and menace, [the producers of the movie] decided

to add a crucial new dimension to the music—sheer volume. . . . [The] producers ran . . . "Rock Around the Clock" wide open, letting the music hit listeners in the gut. In a large theater, "Rock Around the Clock" was loud—for most people, it was the loudest music they had ever heard. The volume of the beat added to the menace . . . aggression, violence. Haley's band may sound quaint when compared to Led Zeppelin or the Sex Pistols, but heavy metal and punk both have their origins in the shock waves produced by the soundtrack of *Blackboard Jungle*.[2]

Those wild, scary shock waves helped make "Rock Around the Clock" the first rock song to top *Billboard*'s pop charts. By the beginning of 1956, "Rock Around the Clock" had sold a phenomenal 6 million copies. No record had ever sold this well, and demand continued for decades, with an estimated 25 million copies sold worldwide. While no exact sales figures for "Rock Around the Clock" exist, a common promotional tagline for the song states it is playing somewhere in the world every minute of every day.

Elvis Is All Shook Up

While Bill Haley rode the rock tidal wave, a new breed of white Southern bad boy was combining the sounds of rock and hillbilly country into a style known as rockabilly. At the center of the rockabilly revolution was Sun Records, a Memphis, Tennessee, recording studio owned by Sam Phillips, a music lover who would lend a sympathetic ear to nearly any blues, bluegrass, or R&B musician who came into his studio. Phillips recorded singles for then-unknown African American blues musicians like B.B. King, Little Milton, Howlin' Wolf, and Ike Turner.

As much as Phillips loved blues music, the widespread racial prejudice of the era prevented him from promoting his records. White-owned radio stations refused to play songs by black musicians, and white store owners would not sell them. The situation forced Phillips to persistently search for a white singer who could sing in the manner of black R&B artists. As his partner Marion Keisker recalled,

"Sam had said, several times, that he wished he could find a white singer with the soul and feeling and the kind of voice to do what was then identified as rhythm & blues songs."[3]

Phillips's wish came true in the spring of 1954, when an eighteen-year-old truck driver named Elvis Presley from Tupelo, Mississippi, entered Sun Studios. There, Presley recorded "That's All Right," a song written in 1946 by blues singer Arthur Crudup. Presley was accompanied by seasoned country performers Scotty Moore on guitar and Bill Black on bass. Although Presley lacked experience, the confidence in his voice and his ringing rhythm guitar sounded unlike anything Phillips had ever heard. "That's All Right" was released in June of 1954, with a rocked-up version of the bluegrass song "Blue Moon of Kentucky" on the other side of the 45 rpm (revolutions per minute) vinyl single.

The choice to release "Blue Moon of Kentucky" was interesting and daring. The song was written and originally recorded in 1946 by bluegrass legend Bill Monroe, who sang it with high hillbilly vocals backed by a fiddle, banjo, guitar, and mandolin. Presley's rocked-up electric adaptation of the country anthem, with his trademark quaky, shaky vocals, might have been considered sacrilegious by country music fans, especially those from Kentucky, but Phillips recognized a bold new sound in Presley's version. It is a melding of hillbilly, blues, and rock that came to be known as rockabilly. Perfected by singer-songwriter Carl Perkins on songs like 1955's "Blue Suede Shoes" (also later recorded by Presley), rockabilly was dangerous, danceable, and became the defining sound of the early rock era.

"Like Busting Out of Jail"

Presley's first single was a minor hit in Memphis, but when he played his songs onstage, he created a sensation unlike any seen before. During a performance, Presley gyrated his hips, wiggled his legs, shook his hair, and jiggled around the

Elvis Presley's dance moves created a sensation and shocked parents.

stage. This created mass hysteria among the teenage girls in the audience, who screamed, yelled, and cried.

Presley's popularity quickly spread by word of mouth, and when he released the emotion-charged "Heartbreak Hotel" on April 21, 1956, it shot to the top of the *Billboard* charts. That song was followed by a string of hits that made Elvis a household name. For 55 of the next 100 weeks, Presley had the best-selling records in America. His gold records—the ones that sold more than a half million copies—included "Hound Dog," "Don't Be Cruel," "All Shook Up," and "Love Me Tender." Most of America, however, was still not ready for Elvis. When he appeared on *The Ed Sullivan Show*, the most popular variety show on television, in 1956, he was shown only from the waist up because his bump-and-grind dancing was deemed too sensual for mass consumption. When asked about the controversy by the media, Presley answered with his trademark politeness and modesty: "I'm not kidding myself. My voice alone is just an ordinary voice. . . . If I stand still while I'm singing, I'm dead, man. I might as well go back to driving a truck."[4]

Despite his humble demeanor offstage, Presley's brand of rockabilly and rock and roll inspired a generation of teenagers. One of these teens, who would one day be known as Bob Dylan, found a unique sense of freedom and rebellion in Presley's music. As Dylan later said about the exhilaration he felt the first time he heard Presley's voice booming from the radio, "I just knew that I wasn't going to work for anybody; nobody was going to be my boss. . . . Hearing [Elvis] for the first time was like busting out of jail."[5]

"Whole Lotta Shakin'"

Until Bill Haley and Elvis Presley came along, there had been no music specifically aimed at teenagers, who were simply expected to listen to the songs that were popular with their parents. And at the time, pop music in America was dominated by syrupy orchestral arrangements and crooning singers wholesomely dressed in sweaters or formal clothes. For example, the week Presley's "Heartbreak Hotel" was released, it competed on the charts with the corny "Hot Diggity" by Perry Como and a sugary instrumental. Other hits at that time included "Love Is a Many Splendored Thing" and "The Yellow Rose of Texas." In such a conservative climate, when Sun Records' alumnus Jerry Lee "Killer" Lewis released the delirious rockabilly hits "Whole Lotta Shakin'" and "Great Balls of Fire" in 1957, he might as well have dropped to Earth from outer space for the effect he had on the teenage audience.

While Elvis's dance moves had shocked parents, nobody was ready for Lewis, who performed in a leopard-skin jacket with his long blond hair flapping in his face. Lewis's onstage antics included physical abuse of his grand pianos. He danced on top, played the upper keys with the heels of his shoes, beat the bass notes with his head, tore off keys and threw them into the audience, and, on occasion, pushed the heavy, expensive instruments off the stage, breaking them into splinters. And there was more, as Lewis once stated: "One night I just filled a Coca-Cola bottle with gasoline and took it [onstage] with me. . . . When I got through doing 'Great Balls of Fire,' I sprinkled some of the gasoline inside the piano and threw a match in. I never could believe a piano could burn like that, but it did."[6]

Driven by his wild stage act, performed in cities across America, "Whole Lotta Shakin'" went to number one on both the country-and-western and R&B charts (there were no rock-and-roll charts at that time). Commenting on his overnight success, one critic wryly noted, "Lewis makes parents mourn for the comparative quiet of [Elvis] Presley."[7] Yet for all of Jerry Lee Lewis's popularity, audiences still expected him to adhere to widely accepted social norms. So when the twenty-three-year-old piano pounder married his fourteen-year-old second cousin in 1958, many Americans were outraged. Although Lewis claimed that such a marriage was not unusual in the rural Louisiana region where he grew up, the explanation did not satisfy indignant Americans who believed that the union was incestuous, and Lewis found his career sidetracked.

Lewis was not the only performer whose antics in front of an audience gave him an almost-mythical status. In Nashville, Tennessee, Gene Vincent gained considerable attention for his pioneering rockabilly sound on hit songs like "Be-Bop-a-Lula," "Race with the Devil," and "Crazy Legs." Vincent's vocals quaked and vibrated harder than Presley's and his appearance foreshadowed the rock star image that would become commonplace in later decades. Vincent was the first rocker to dress from head to toe in black leather, he had a nasty limp from a motorcycle accident, and he put forth a menacing swagger onstage while holding his mouth twisted into a sneer. Just as punk rockers would do decades later, Vincent thrashed about while singing, leaping from amps and writhing on his back.

Rave On

Gene Vincent and Jerry Lee Lewis perfected enduring bad-boy rockabilly images that stood in complete contrast to the clean-cut Buddy Holly. Born in 1936 in Lubbock, Texas, Holly was raised playing country music by icons like Hank Williams, the Delmore Brothers, and the Louvin Brothers. By the time he was twenty, Holly was a regular performer at local dance halls, bars, and on local radio, with sets that combined country with rock and rockabilly. Although Holly's trademark thick-framed glasses, skinny ties, and suit coats made him look more like a handsome high school math teacher, he had already emerged as one of rockabilly's most talented singer-songwriters.

Working with his band the Crickets, Holly produced a rhythm-heavy rock sound and catchy melodies that propelled him to stardom in 1957 after the release of a string of hit singles that included "That'll Be the Day," "Peggy Sue," "Not Fade Away," and "Rave On."

It is often said that at the height of his meteoric career, Holly told an interviewer, "Death is very often referred to as a good career move."[8] He was kidding, but his words proved to be prophetic. On a freezing February 3, 1959, after a gig in Clear Lake, Iowa, an airplane carrying Buddy Holly and two other rock musicians, Richie Valens and J.P. Richardson, crashed into an Iowa cornfield, killing all three. Although Holly was only twenty-three, he left a legacy of influential music that did not fade away throughout the decades.

Rock-and-Roll Backlash

The suggestive lyrics and stage moves of Jerry Lee Lewis, Elvis Presley, and Little Richard drew scorn from national critics. Rock journalists Linda Martin and Kerry Segrave describe the backlash against rock and roll fueled by frightened parents and crusading reporters:

In April 1956 the mass circulation paper, the *New York Daily News*, ran a two-part series slamming rock as an "inciter of juvenile delinquency." . . . The series even then was predicting the death of rock mainly because "disgusted adults were battling the music of delinquents." According to the writer, Jess Stearn, it had taken a lot to set off this adult revolt, "riots and bloodshed, slurs on the national anthem, and slowly gathering public disgust at a barrage of primitive jungle-beat rhythms, which when set to lyrics at all, frequently sound off with double meaning leer-ics few adults would care to hear."

The editors of *Music Journal* were much more horrified and revolted by the specter of rock and roll. The magazine considered it to be its "duty" to comment on "the most disgraceful blasphemy ever committed in the name of music." The music was savage, illiterate, and vicious and the link between the music and juvenile delinquency was overwhelmingly clear.

Linda Martin and Kerry Segrave. *Anti-Rock*. Hamden, CT: Archon Books, 1988, pp. 52–53.

Little Richard and the Upsetters

Fifties rockers like Buddy Holly, Elvis Presley, and Gene Vincent presented African American music styles to white teenagers. This led many white rock fans to seek out records by black artists. Among African American musicians, no one delivered the frenzied, hard-charging sound of black rock and roll better than "Little Richard" Penniman.

Born in 1932, Little Richard got his start singing in the church choir as a child. But when he started to play rock and roll with his band, the Upsetters, Little Richard did Jerry Lee Lewis one better, dressing in outrageously glitzy outfits, wearing a tall pompadour hairdo, and lightening his face with makeup. As drummer Charles Conner later recalled, the band's name, the Upsetters, "wasn't just a name; when we'd go into a place, we'd upset it! We were the first band on the road to wear pancake makeup and eye shadow, have an earring hanging out of our ear and have our hair curled."[9]

During the highly conservative 1950s, Little Richard's barely concealed homosexuality was considered as bold as his music. Few teenagers seemed to know or care about his sexual orientation, and Little Richard's singles, such as "Long Tall Sally," "Slippin' and Slidin'," "Ready Teddy," and especially "Good Golly Miss Molly" and "Tutti Frutti," which were all released between 1955 and 1957, became instant rock classics. Shrieking his trademark head-shaking "Whooo!" and hammering out the boogie-woogie rhythm on the piano, Little Richard added new vocabulary to teen slang when he howled the famous opening line to "Tutti Frutti": "Awhop-bob-a-loo-mop! Alop-bam-boom!"[10]

The Rock-and-Roll Poet

Little Richard's brand of rock and roll came down to a driving beat and simple, suggestively catchy words. But right in the midst of this flamboyant rock rebellion, a hairdresser from St. Louis, Missouri, named Chuck Berry added an intellectual aspect to the music and, in doing so, became the first rock-and-roll poet.

Berry wrote songs about cars, boredom with high school, guitars, young love, and, of course, rock-and-roll music itself. They were topics every 1950s American teenager understood. Berry started each song with the same hot guitar lick that came to symbolize rock and roll in those early years. Onstage he would perform his famous duckwalk,

Chuck Berry performs his famous "duck walk" on stage.

loping along with one knee bent and the other leg out front pulling him across the stage, all the while strumming his guitar.

Berry's songs "Johnny B. Goode," "Maybellene," "Roll Over Beethoven," "Sweet Little Sixteen," "Memphis," and "Rock and Roll Music" shone with joyous—and smart— rock-and-roll poetry. In "Maybellene," Berry sings about "motivating over the hill" when he sees "Maybellene in a Coupe de Ville." And although the Cadillac was rolling on the open road, nothing could outrun his big Ford.

Berry's intelligent and intricate wordplay was tailored for his audience, as he explained in a December 2001 interview with *Rolling Stone* magazine: "I wrote about cars because half the people had cars, or wanted them. I wrote about love, because everybody wants that. I wrote songs white people could buy, because that's nine pennies out of every dime. That was my goal: to look at my bankbook and see a million dollars there."[11]

Berry made his million, but by 1960, rock and roll had fallen on hard times. Elvis Presley was drafted into the army in 1958, and that same year Little Richard found religion, renounced his rock-and-roll lifestyle, and (temporarily) quit the entertainment business to preach the gospel. Chuck Berry was imprisoned for transporting an underage girl across state lines (he claimed he was set up by police), Buddy Holly was gone, and Jerry Lee Lewis's career was in ruins. While rock and roll was only seven years old, its founding fathers were dead or missing. The situation prompted Bing Crosby, one of the most popular singers from the World War II era, to proclaim, "Rock 'n' Roll seems to have run its course. . . . [It will be replaced by] slow, pretty ballads."[12] While rock fans scoffed, the future of rock music seemed to be slippin' and slidin' away.

Sixties Rock and Roll, Folk, and Soul

In 1960 the careers of rock's founding fathers had peaked and most were no longer making records. Some critics pronounced rock and roll dead, as a group of clean-cut white teenage crooners such as Pat Boone, Fabian, Frankie Avalon, and Paul Anka dominated the pop charts.

The predictions of rock's demise proved to be premature. The style with roots in Tennessee, Louisiana, and Texas had become an international phenomenon. Rock's influence was being felt from the Midwest to London, England, and even in the drab working-class city of Liverpool, England.

Although Liverpool was unknown to the vast majority of people in the United States, a group of talented young Liverpudlians was about to take the world by storm, enshrine rock music to a permanent place in history, and change the way people looked, talked, and even thought.

The band was the Beatles, and its members, guitarist John Lennon, bassist Paul McCartney, lead guitar player George Harrison, and drummer Ringo Starr, started out playing songs by Little Richard, Chuck Berry, Gene Vincent, Buddy Holly, and other rock originals. Instead of copying the music directly, though, the Beatles put their own spin on it, throwing in occasional jazz chords and singing with an almost angelic three-part harmony that had previously been lacking in most rock songs. In addition to playing rock standards, Lennon and McCartney wrote their own music, which sounded unlike anything anyone had ever heard.

The Lads from Liverpool

The roots of the Beatles can be traced to 1957, when John Lennon and Paul McCartney, both still in high school, first played together. After several years of local gigs, the Beatles were booked to an extended engagement in the notorious red-light district of Hamburg, Germany, in 1960. The group played at bars in an area known as the Reeperbahn, which was filled with seedy music clubs, live sex shows, prostitutes, transvestites, and drunken sailors. Fueled by amphetamines and beer, the Beatles played up to ten hours a night, seven days a week. To stave off boredom, and to please the rowdy crowds, the group experimented musically. As Lennon later recalled: "In Hamburg we had to play for hours and hours on end. Every song lasted twenty minutes and had twenty solos in it. . . . That's what improved the playing. And the Germans like heavy rock, so you have to keep rocking all the time; that's how we got stomping."[13]

The Beatles' exuberant music attracted a crowd of sophisticated local art students and philosophers. One who came to hear the Beatles perform was Astrid Kirchherr, an artist, photographer, and fashion designer who, with her camera, made musical history. Kirchherr recorded some of the earliest images of the Beatles as a group. She also talked the band into abandoning their greasy Elvis-style pompadours in favor of the "French cut" style, in which the hair was allowed to fall over the ears and was trimmed neatly all around, creating a kind of "moptop." At a time when men almost universally wore their hair trimmed short, the Beatles' hairdos were considered a radical, even rebellious, look.

"Awesome Firepower and Tightness"

Eventually, the Beatles returned to Liverpool, and their newly developed sound helped them land a gig playing daily lunch-hour shows at a basement club called the

Cavern. Over the next several years, the Beatles attracted an ever-growing crowd of fourteen-year-old girls, office workers, and secretaries in short skirts and beehive hairdos, who packed into the club during their lunch breaks. Some of these young women carried large purses with homemade embroidered messages that read "I Love You John," "I Love Paul," and "I Love the Beatles."[14]

Onstage, the band had an unusual stage presence. Instead of putting a professional face on their well-crafted music, they fooled around, eating lunch, smoking, and joking with each other and the audience between songs. John Lennon's boyhood friend, Pete Shotten, describes the band's quick-witted antics onstage:

John, with his lifelong inability to remember lyrics, often ended up ad-libbing the words to his favorite rock & roll classics, peppering the familiar melody with obscenities, in-jokes, and snatches of his inimitable gobbledegook. As often as not, the results singularly failed to fit the song's original meter, and the Beatles rendition would peter out in a chorus of laughter. . . . This evident spontaneity—coupled with the awesome firepower and tightness of the band when it did get down to business . . . enabled the Beatles to regularly eclipse all other . . . bands who preceded or followed them onto the Cavern [a club in Liverpool] stage.[15]

In 1961, as the Beatles endeared themselves to an expanding audience, they hooked up with Brian Epstein, a twenty-seven-year-old record-store owner who became their manager. Although he was inexperienced as a promoter of musicians, Epstein propelled the Beatles towards stardom through sheer dogged determination. He made them clean up their act by giving up eating, smoking, and swearing onstage, and he dressed them in suits and ties. Meanwhile, the band began to write their own songs, which allowed them to showcase their talent individually. Lennon and McCartney were a particularly potent songwriting team, and early songs such as "Love Me Do," "PS I Love You," and "Ask Me Why" are excellent vehicles for showcasing the band's tight vocal harmonies and instrumental talent during live performances.

The Beatles' obvious talent, coupled with Epstein's promotion, eventually caught the attention of a major record label. In August 1962, the Beatles were awarded a contract with Parlophone Records, a subsidiary of the prestigious EMI record company. Parlophone's in-house music producer was George Martin, a classically trained pianist whose background was producing light orchestral music. With his scholarly understanding of 1960s recording equipment and his ability to write unique horn and string arrangements, Martin's musical influence combined with the talents of the Beatles in an exceptional synergy that changed the sound of rock and roll.

Into the Top Twenty

By the autumn of 1962 the Beatles' first single, "Love Me Do," was selling briskly in Liverpool, and those sales lifted the single onto the British list of top-twenty hits. The group followed up this success with two more Lennon/McCartney compositions, "Please Please Me" and "From Me to You." Both rocketed to number one within days of their release. These hit singles were later included on the Beatles' first long-playing (LP) album *Please Please Me*, recorded in a marathon ten-hour session on February 11, 1963.

The band's talent was well displayed on *Please Please Me*. Now classic Lennon/McCartney tunes such as "I Saw Her Standing There" demonstrate the group's penchant for soaring three-part harmony, and the song "Do You Want to Know a Secret" shows that the group could write songs that even parents could love. Upon its release, *Please Please Me* immediately went to the top of the LP charts, staying there a record-breaking twenty-nine weeks. Little more than a year after meeting Brian Epstein, the Beatles had become the hottest act in the British Isles.

When the band's fourth single, "She Loves You," was released in August 1963, the "yeah, yeah, yeah" chorus had millions of young people singing along with "the Fab Four," and the Beatles' look was all the rage. By this time, nearly every schoolboy in Britain was cutting his hair in the mop-top fashion of John, Paul, George, and Ringo. Stores that sold pointy ankle-high boots with stacked heels, or "Beatle boots," could not keep them in stock.

Americans Catch Beatlemania

The invasion of the United States by British rock and roll began in December 1963, when the Beatles released the song "I Want to Hold Your Hand" in Britain and it quickly sold a million copies and went to number one. Days later, James Carroll, a disc jockey (DJ) in Washington, D.C., played a copy of the song that he had picked up overseas. Within minutes, the station's phones began ringing nonstop with hundreds of requests for the song to be played again. Other radio stations across the country obtained advance copies of the song from Capitol Records, and when it was released in the United States on December 25, it sold a million copies within days. One month later, "She Loves You" was

The Beatles' appearance on The Ed Sullivan Show *helped make them the most popular band in the United States after achieving great success in Britain.*

released, and it too went to number one on the *Billboard* charts, making it the first time any artist had two consecutive chart toppers.

When young Americans heard the band and saw their pictures in national magazines, hysteria for the band, known as Beatlemania, broke out as quickly as it had in Britain. The band was booked to play on *The Ed Sullivan Show*, the most popular variety show on television at the time, for two consecutive weekends, February 9 and 16, 1964. The show received fifty thousand requests for tickets to the Beatles' performance in the seven-hundred-seat theater from which it was broadcast.

More than 73 million Americans—almost half the country—watched the Beatles on *The Ed Sullivan Show*. When the boys sang "Woooo!" and shook their long hair during "She Loves You," the teary-eyed teenage girls in the audience erupted in shrieks and screams that overwhelmed the sound system. By that March, the Beatles had become the hottest band in America.

Searching for New Sounds

As the new kings of rock and roll, the Beatles had fame that quickly spread around the world. But instead of sticking with the musical formula that won them success, the band experimented with new styles. Still, the Beatles continued to please their listeners. Working on a tight schedule, they released two critically acclaimed, best-selling albums every year, including *A Hard Day's Night*, *Beatles for Sale*, and *Help!*

On the album *Rubber Soul*, the Beatles reinvented their music once again, forging a dynamic blend of sweet acoustic guitars, jangling electric guitars, and lilting bass lines that were unique in pop music. George Harrison added to the mix by playing a traditional Indian stringed instrument known as a sitar on John Lennon's song "Norwegian Wood." This was the first time that the sitar was heard by most rock fans, but not the last. Soon dozens of other bands, including the Rolling Stones, began to use the sound of the sitar layered within their rock songs.

A Hard Day's Night

During the Beatlemania era, there were only three television networks in the United States, and the mass media was limited to broadcast television, radio, magazines, and newspapers. There was no MTV, Internet, twenty-four-hour entertainment networks, or any other way for hungry Beatles fans to stay in touch with the band that they loved. So when the a-day-in-the-life-of-the-Beatles movie *A Hard Day's Night* premiered in June 1964, Beatles fans all over the world were able to get an inside look at their favorite band for the first time.

A Hard Day's Night opened in five hundred American movie theaters and grossed $1.3 million in its first week.

More than a business success, the movie certified the Beatles as bona fide movie stars and added to their legend. The shots of the Beatles traveling, hanging around backstage, and answering fan mail in hotel rooms also helped moviegoers bond with the band. It was also the first true music video ever filmed, with "jump cuts" of the band leaping through the air, running wildly across empty fields, playing live concerts before screaming audiences, and being chased through London's streets by teenage girls. The movie is now considered a classic, and movie critic Roger Ebert even taught it to his film classes, analyzing it for his students one shot at a time.

Folk Music Meets Rock and Roll

The songs on *Rubber Soul* blended sensitive, introspective lyrics, acoustic folk music, and rock and roll. This new sound was referred to as folk rock, a sound pioneered by Bob Dylan. Born Robert Zimmerman in Hibbing, Minnesota, in 1941, Dylan hitchhiked to New York City in 1961 and soon became a fixture in the Greenwich Village folk music scene. While most folk singers of the era re-created folk and blues songs in their original form, Dylan wrote his own music combining country, folk, blues, and rock. Within a year, Dylan was signed to the prestigious Columbia Records for a five-album deal.

Dylan released the album *The Freewheelin' Bob Dylan* in 1963, and it overflowed with a new form of music. Dylan songs such as "Blowin' in the Wind" and "A Hard Rain's A-Gonna Fall" are intricate, wordy, and evoke surrealistic,

and sometimes harsh poetic imagery never before found in popular music. When his follow-up album *The Times They Are A-Changin'* was released in 1964, Dylan was branded a genius by critics, who called him the voice of the new generation.

As music journalist Michael Gray writes, Dylan's most dedicated fans were "students and liberals who considered themselves radicals, hated pop music and wore Dylan on their sleeves like a political armband."[16] Therefore, many of Dylan's fans were aghast when, in 1965, he famously "went electric" with the release of *Bringing It All Back Home*. From the first notes on the album, Dylan rips into his songs with a Fender Stratocaster guitar in hand, backed by a jangling rock ensemble.

As critics howled, Dylan's bitingly satirical and humorous side came to the fore with hilarious wordplay on songs such as "Subterranean Homesick Blues" and "Bob Dylan's 115th Dream." Proving he could not be pinned down to one style, Dylan also performed several hauntingly beautiful acoustic songs on *Bringing It All Back Home*, such as the classics "Mr. Tambourine Man," "Gates of Eden," and "(It's All Over Now) Baby Blue."

Despite the musical mix, many fans refused to accept the new Dylan sound. His fans believed, as Michael Gray writes, "[He] was this folk singer committing the ultimate sacrilege of singing rock 'n' roll songs with electric guitars behind him. Students—serious-minded young people unaware of the social upheavals about to happen—were appalled that Dylan should resort to such triviality."[17] When Dylan played songs from the album at the Newport Folk Festival in Newport, Rhode Island, he was loudly booed and organizers threatened to unplug his amp.

Emotional Masterpieces

Dylan, only recently the golden boy of the folk scene, was angry. His next album, *Highway 61 Revisited*, reflected his emotions in songs such "Like a Rolling Stone." Clocking in at more than six minutes long, "Like a Rolling Stone" was, at the time, the longest song ever released on a 45 rpm single, and the first to break the three-minute "barrier" to which radio programmers traditionally adhered.

Dylan's next album was a double-record set, *Blonde on Blonde*, which brought his album total to eight sides of vinyl in two years. This masterpiece contains another round of classics that, for many listeners, still sounds fresh today. Timeless love songs such as "I Want You" and "Just Like a Woman" permeate the album between hallucinatory

The Jingle-Jangle of Folk Rock

Although critics were disappointed when Bob Dylan went electric on *Bringing It All Back Home*, the rock band the Byrds had a number-one hit when they electrified "Mr. Tambourine Man," one of the acoustic numbers from Dylan's album. With angelic three-part harmonies spinning Dylan's dream-like words, "Mr. Tambourine Man" blends folk music with rock so well that "folk rock" became a well-defined style of music practically overnight.

The success of folk rock was seized upon by several groups looking to combine the personally expressive words of Dylan with the bright guitar and harmony work of the Beatles. Most of the bands who were successful brought something of their own creative inspiration into the music. The Mamas and Papas was one such group. This foursome of folk rock superstars produced a string of hit singles, including "California Dreamin," "Monday Monday," and the autobiographical "Creeque Alley."

Other stars of the folk rock movement included Buffalo Springfield, the Lovin' Spoonful, the Turtles, and Donovan. While some folk rockers, such as Simon and Garfunkel, went on to rewarding careers, the folk rock sensation only lasted a few years before psychedelic rock came to dominate the pop charts.

masterpieces such as "Visions of Johanna" and "Stuck Inside of Mobile with the Memphis Blues Again." Dylan toured the world in 1965 and 1966, singing the songs from his recent burst of prolific creativity. Backed by an electric group known simply as The Band, Dylan was booed by some, adulated as a rock god by others, and incessantly hounded by the press, who kept pinning the "protest singer" label on him long after he had moved on musically. Parts of the tour were captured in the critically acclaimed 1967 film *Don't Look Back*.

While there has never been a shortage of criticism and scorn during every phase of Dylan's career, he continues to make original, creative, and poetic music to this day. In 2011 the seventy-year-old Dylan continued to play concerts across the globe and performed for the first time in Vietnam and China.

Over the course of nearly fifty years, Bob Dylan recorded forty-five albums. He provided a living illustration of how rock and roll can be an ever-changing, looping musical form that may be shaped and reshaped to suit the performer's mood. As one of the most important songwriters in rock history, Dylan inspired everyone from the Beatles to hip-hop artist Eminem.

The Rolling Stones embraced African American blues music and became the most successful of the British Invasion bands.

The British Blues Invasion

Bob Dylan's mid-1960s music was made during an era known as the British Invasion. The success of the Beatles in the United States paved the way for other British rock bands, including the Rolling Stones, the Kinks, the Yardbirds, and the Who.

Many of the groups that were part of the British Invasion were strongly influenced by blues music. Ironically, these British groups embraced African American music with a much greater passion than bands in the United States, where blues was born. The Rolling Stones were the most successful British Invasion band, and they took their cues from blues players like Howlin' Wolf, Little Walter, Elmore James, and Muddy Waters. In the blues tradition, the Stones salted their songs with aggressive guitar licks and loud, driving rhythms. The group's 1965 hit "(I Can't Get No) Satisfaction," landed them a coveted gig on *The Ed Sullivan Show*, and the group produced number-one songs every year well into the twenty-first century.

Sweet Sixties Soul

In addition to blues music, the Rolling Stones were heavily influenced by the soul music of Aretha Franklin, James Brown, Martha and the Vandellas, and Smokey Robinson. These, along with other African American performers, provided some of the only competition for the Beatles and British Invasion bands during the mid-1960s.

Soul, with its roots in spirituals and gospel music, was modernized R&B. Ray Charles, one of the founding fathers of soul, wrote songs with blues lyrics layered over traditional gospel melodies, adding boogie-woogie keyboard flourishes to the mix. Charles's musical genius allowed him to produce hits nearly every year during the 1960s, including "What'd I Say," "Georgia," "Hit the Road Jack," "Let's Go Get Stoned," and a deeply soulful reworking of the country song "I Can't Stop Loving You," which sold more than 3 million copies. By the 1970s, Charles was an international star, widely recognized for his musical contributions to the American songbook.

Hitsville, U.S.A.

While Ray Charles was a solo artist, some of the sweetest soul sounds were produced by a community of talented

singers, songwriters, and musicians in Detroit, Michigan. They recorded for a former Ford autoworker named Berry Gordy, who started a company called Motown Records in a small bungalow on West Grand Boulevard. Marked only by a sign that read "Hitsville, U.S.A.," the unassuming dwelling was ground zero for the Motown musical explosion that provided an urban sound track to the 1960s.

In its early days, Motown relied on other, larger record companies to promote and distribute its records. After achieving minor success with singles by a few R&B groups,

Smokey Robinson and the Miracles were the first success at Motown Records after the company decided to distribute its own musicians.

Gordy released "Bad Girl," sung by Smokey Robinson and backed by a group called the Miracles. "Bad Girl" was distributed by Chess Records, but after the song reached number ninety-three on the national charts, Robinson convinced Gordy that Motown could make a lot more money if it distributed its own records. Against the advice of his lawyers, who warned that record distribution was too expensive of an undertaking, Gordy pressed ahead and beat the odds with a number-two hit titled "Shop Around," co-written with Robinson and distributed by Motown.

Flush with success, Motown signed a number of female singers. Their resulting popularity would be a major part of what was known as the girl-group style, in which young women harmonized on songs about love and their ideal boyfriends. Motown capitalized on this fad, charting hit after hit with acts like Mary Wells ("Two Lovers," "My Guy"), the Marvelettes ("Please, Mr. Postman"), and Martha and the Vandellas ("Heat Wave," "Dancing in the Streets").

Motown soul music was driven by a hot house band called the Funk Brothers, who played on nearly every song. The Funk Brothers filled songs with short, tasteful saxophone riffs and an impeccable rhythm section featuring jangling pianos, crisp staccato guitar chords, bouncing bass, chiming tambourine, and backbeat-heavy snare drums that made listeners want to snap their fingers, tap their feet, and dance.

"The Sound of Young America"

The success of Motown lay not only in the talents of its musicians and singers, but also in its songwriters. The label's star songwriting team featured Lamont Dozier, who worked with brothers Brian and Eddie Holland. The so-called Holland-Dozier-Holland (H-D-H) team created an unprecedented line of immortal hits that continued to receive major airplay decades after their creation. A few of their many hits released between 1964 and 1967 include "Baby I Need Your Loving," "I Can't Help Myself," "It's the Same Old Song," and "Reach Out, I'll Be There" for the Four Tops; "Can I Get a Witness" and "How Sweet It Is

Motown Finishing School

During an era in which bloody inner-city riots and the rise of the black power movement made many whites suspicious or even antagonistic toward any manifestation of African American culture, Motown founder Berry Gordy sought to teach the singers how to project an image of elegance and grace. He felt that this would gain his acts the widest audience. To facilitate this goal, I.T.M. (International Talent Management) hired Maxine Powell, who owned a finishing and modeling school, to groom Motown artists. Powell described her work:

The singers were raw. . . . They were from the streets, and like most of us who came out of the [housing] projects, they were a little crude: some were backward, some were arrogant. They had potential, but they were not unlike their friends in the ghetto. I always thought of our artists as diamonds in the rough who needed polishing. . . . Many of them had abusive tones of voice, so I had to teach them how to speak in a nonthreatening manner. . . . Many of them slouched, so I had to show them what posture meant. Some were temperamental and moody; I would lecture them about their attitude. . . . I chose which clothes were best for them as well. We used to call them "uniforms." . . . And on stage technique, I taught them little things like never turning their backs to an audience, never protruding their buttocks onstage. . . . We really wanted young blacks to understand that you do not have to look like you came out of the ghetto in order to be somebody other blacks and even whites would respect when you made it big.

Quoted in David P. Szatmary. *Rockin' in Time: A Social History of Rock and Roll.* New York: Schirmer Books, 1996, pp. 130–131.

(To Be Loved By You)" for Marvin Gaye; "Heat Wave" and "Nowhere to Run" for Martha and the Vandellas; and their biggest-selling songs, "You Can't Hurry Love," "Baby Love," "Come See About Me," "Stop! In the Name of Love," "You Keep Me Hanging On," and "I Hear a Symphony" for the Supremes. Rock journalists Joe McEwan and Jim Miller explain the Holland-Dozier-Holland hit-making formula:

As soul producers, they were little short of revolutionary. The trio rarely used standard song forms, opting instead for a simpler, more direct . . . pattern, anchored

Aretha Franklin Demands R-E-S-P-E-C-T

The civil rights movement of the early sixties gave a measure of political clout to African Americans for the first time in the twentieth century. As young African Americans flexed their new political muscle, Aretha Franklin tapped into the spirit of the times by spelling out R-E-S-P-E-C-T, in her 1967 hit "Respect." Rock journalist Gillian G. Gaar explains the song's impact:

"Respect" was followed into the Top 10 by . . . "(You Make Me Feel Like) A Natural Woman" and the LP *Aretha Arrives.* . . . By the end of the decade Aretha Franklin was clearly one of America's top female singers and an international star.

Gillian G. Gaar. She's a Rebel: The History of Women In Rock & Roll. New York: Seal Press, 1992, p. 79.

"Respect" hit a potent nerve in 1967. . . . Riots broke out in the black neighborhoods of several cities across America throughout the summer. . . . Newspapers, periodicals and television commentators pondered the question of 'Why?' as Aretha Franklin spelled it all out in one word, *R-E-S-P-E-C-T!* . . . *Ebony* writer David Llorens dubbed 1967 "the summer of 'Retha, Rap and Revolt!" But "Respect"'s broad appeal was also due to the fact that the song could be read in a number of different ways. "It could be a racial situation, it could be a political situation, it could be just the man-woman situation," Tom Dowd, the recording engineer for the song, told *Rolling Stone,* adding, "Anybody could identify with it. It cut a lot of ground." . . .

Aretha Franklin's song "Respect" gained broad appeal during the tumultuous late 60s because it could be interpreted as a comment on the racial, political, or women's rights movements of the time.

by an endless refrain of the song's hook line. The effect of this [circular] structure was cumulative, giving Holland-Dozier-Holland productions a compulsive momentum. [And] each and every one of them was immediately familiar, subtly distinctive and quite unforgettable. . . . If the vocalists provided emotion, the band mounted a nonstop percussive assault highlighted by a "hot" mix, with shrill, hissing cymbals and a booming bass—anything to make a song jump out of a car radio. With tambourines rattling to a blistering 4/4 beat, the H-D-H sound, introduced on "Heat Wave" and perfected on records like the Four Tops' "Reach Out, I'll Be There" and the Supremes' "You Can't Hurry Love" (both from 1966), came to epitomize what Motown would call "The Sound of Young America."[18]

The importance of sixties soul went beyond just the music. Some of the soul groups, such as the Temptations and the Supremes, were nearly as popular as the Beatles, representing the first time that black artists had gained such widespread acceptance among white audiences. This came at a time when Martin Luther King Jr. had become a household name and his speeches were inspiring millions of Americans, both black and white, to dream of a day when justice and equality would triumph over prejudice and discrimination. For many Americans, the sound of the dream was provided by Smokey Robinson, the Supremes, Martha and the Vandellas, Stevie Wonder, the Temptations, and Marvin Gaye.

Motown created a well-oiled soul-music machine. Seventy-five percent of the company's records listed in the top 100 on the national record charts, and the label's hits blasted out of nearly every radio in the 1960s. Along with Beatlemania and Bob Dylan's innovative folk rock, soul was part of the complex and turbulent musical scene that dominated rock and roll during the first half of the 1960s.

CHAPTER 3

Rock Gets Experienced

The 1960s was one of the most turbulent and transformational decades in history. By 1966 so many forces of change were spinning at once it was often difficult to tell if society was improving or about to collapse into chaos. While some were chanting for peace and love, there were bloody riots in hundreds of cities, and violent protests against the unpopular Vietnam War. Some preached that marijuana and the psychedelic drug LSD (lysergic acid diethylamide or acid) could save the world, while thousands of young people, including many rock stars, drank to excess and experimented with deadly and addictive drugs, including heroin. Issues of war, peace, love, hate, drugs, sex, and freedom were endlessly discussed in the media and around dining room tables across America. For the first time, these topics were also addressed in popular songs that became part of the modern cultural fabric of the country.

This social upheaval became a revolution known as the hippie, or counterculture, movement. In 1967 the movement peaked during what became known in the media as the Summer of Love. At the epicenter of the hippie movement was the Haight-Ashbury neighborhood in San Francisco, California, a run-down area where affordable apartments butted up against the beautiful natural wonders of Golden Gate Park. In the Haight, long-haired hippies dressed in brightly colored tie-dyed clothes, sandals, and love beads. They held "love-ins" with live music meant to promote world peace and the liberation of the human spirit from the confines of what they referred to as the "straight" world. Singer-songwriter David Crosby, of Crosby, Stills & Nash, observed that adults had little chance of slowing the counterculture movement:

> On one side you got war; degradation, death, submission, guilt, fear, competition; and on the other hand you got a bunch of people lyin' out on the beach, walking around in the sun, laughin', playin' music, makin' love and gettin' high, singin', dancin', wearin' bright colors, tellin' stories, livin' pretty easy. You offer that alternative to a kid, man, and the kid ain't crazy yet. I think that they've probably lost the majority of their kids by now.[19]

The Beatles' Artistic Pursuit

The swirling psychedelic sound track for the Summer of Love came from the most popular rock band in the world, the Beatles. On June 1, 1967, the band released the album *Sgt. Pepper's Lonely Hearts Club Band*. It was the first rock "concept" album—one in which all of the songs were related to one another musically and thematically. *Sgt. Pepper* was also one of the first albums to open to double size, and the first to have song lyrics printed on it. Commenting on the importance of the album, producer George Martin explains that *Sgt. Pepper* succeeded in "speaking for its age, capturing the sixties and much of what that era came to stand for in sound: the psychedelia, the fashions, the vogue for Eastern mysticism, the spirit of adventure, the whole peace and love thing, the anti-war movement; it was all there and more."[20]

Sgt. Pepper was released during a time of prolific musical exploration by the Beatles. Between late 1966 and the end of 1967, the Beatles produced a string of psychedelic hit singles including "Strawberry Fields Forever," "I Am the Walrus," "Penny Lane," and "Yellow Submarine." These musical collages prompted *Village Voice* rock critic Richard Goldstein to presciently write in 1967, "We will view [this

"Strawberry Fields Forever"

After the Beatles began experimenting with psychedelic drugs, the group began to spend months in the studio working on a single song, using unusual instruments and manipulating recording equipment in extraordinary ways. One of the first songs produced in this manner was "Strawberry Fields Forever," a whimsical and dream-like John Lennon composition that contrasts the unreality of the drug experience with childhood memories.

Producer George Martin framed "Strawberry Fields Forever" with tape loops and an extremely primitive electric synthesizer called a Mellotron, and added a swirling "sound picture" marked by recordings of Ringo Starr's drum cymbals played backwards. Martin, the band, and studio musicians also supplemented the sound with trumpets, cellos, and a harp-like Indian instrument called a swarmandal, played by George Harrison. In *With a Little Help from My Friends: The Making of Sgt. Pepper*, Martin gives his opinion of the musical masterpiece:

> Way ahead of its time, strong, complicated both in concept and execution, highly original and quickly labeled "psychedelic," "Strawberry Fields Forever" was the work of an undoubted genius. We could not have produced a better prototype for the future. . . . We were all very proud of our new baby. For my money, it was the most original and inventive track to date in pop music.

George Martin. *With a Little Help from My Friends: The Making of Sgt. Pepper*. New York: Little, Brown and Company, 1994, p. 24.

music] in retrospect as key [works] in the development of rock 'n' roll into an artistic pursuit."[21]

Much of the Beatles' artistry occurred in the recording studio. Although they still made records on four-track reel-to-reel tape equipment, they piled sound over sound on the same small piece of recording tape. Songs were filled with backward guitar licks, distortion, filters, and unconventional musical instruments. The rich aural effects of these "tape loops," or samples, was later made possible by transistorized "effects pedals." In the 1980s, digital sampling devices did the work, and in the 1990s, computers were used to manipulate sound. In 1967, however, it was up to the Beatles to "invent" dozens of new sounds with analog equipment little different than that used by musicians in the 1950s.

Psychedelic San Francisco

The evolution of rock and roll into art permanently changed the sound of music. The Beatles' success gave bands permission to explore the outer boundaries of rock music, and nowhere was this more evident than in Haight-Ashbury. Fueled by marijuana, acid, hallucinogenic mushrooms, and other drugs, several San Francisco bands emerged in the mid-sixties that made the pre-psychedelic Beatles look quaint, tame, and old-fashioned by comparison. Like many rockers of the era, these musicians had roots in folk music. For example, Jerry Garcia, lead guitarist of the Grateful Dead, began his career as a banjo player whose repertoire included many traditional old-time country songs. Paul Kantner, the founder of Jefferson Airplane, was a regular at San Francisco sing-along parties called hootenannies. Another Airplane member, Marty Balin, owned the Matrix, a nightclub that featured folk music.

The Grateful Dead's Molecular Evolution

The San Francisco music scene got a major boost in 1965 when Ken Kesey, author of the classic best seller *One Flew Over the Cuckoo's Nest*, held a series of "acid tests." At these events, LSD—which was still legal at the time—was given to hundreds of people who decorated their bodies with Day-Glo paint, watched protoplasmic light shows, and danced all night long to the psychedelic rock of the Grateful Dead. Kesey's acid tests spread LSD use far and wide, and the psychedelic revolution quickly overtook America. Jerry Garcia described his reasons for partaking: "To get really high is

The Grateful Dead fused country, jazz, blues, folk, and bluegrass to form a new brand of music that some critics referred to as acid jazz.

to forget yourself. . . . And to forget yourself is to see everything else. And to see everything else is to become an understanding molecule in evolution, a conscious tool in the universe."[22]

As the "house band" for the acid tests, the Dead fused country, blues, jazz, and bluegrass on electric instruments, and formed a new brand of music sometimes called acid jazz, because it relies on the improvisation and free-form expression found in jazz music. Social critic Charles Perry comments on this new sound:

Most of the rock musicians in San Francisco were basically folkies learning how to play electrified instruments. . . . They had a tentative sound at first and played a lot of solemn, chiming chords on the beat. When it came time for the guitarist to take a solo break, he often noodled up and down the notes of the scale in a way that might owe as much to inexperience in improvisation as it did to the influence of [traditional music].[23]

Swooping and Soaring

The music may have been tentative at first, but the Grateful Dead recorded classic albums that mixed acid rock with jazzy folk overtones. While their first several albums, *Anthem of the Sun* and *Aoxomoxoa*, are psychedelic masterpieces, later records such as *Workingman's Dead* and *American Beauty* are loaded with folky three-part harmony, ringing acoustic guitars, and understated leads by Garcia.

Like most San Francisco bands, the Dead could best be appreciated live, and they themselves admit they never captured their true sound on records. As a result, the Dead toured relentlessly for nearly thirty years, keeping the sixties counterculture movement alive among hundreds of thousands of dedicated fans until the death of Jerry Garcia in 1995. The Dead also invented the jam band concept celebrated in later decades by Phish, the Dave Matthews Band, and others. Jam bands rarely play a song the same way twice. Each rendition is inherently different because of musical improvisation (or jams).

While the Dead continued to rock throughout the 1960s, the careers of other San Francisco bands burned hot and fast. Jefferson Airplane was one of the first Bay Area bands to sign a major recording deal, and the first to have a string of number-one hits. When the band released the album *Surrealistic Pillow* in 1967, music fans across the globe were able to hear the San Francisco sound echoing through songs like "Somebody to Love" and "White Rabbit," the latter of which was based on the storybook *Alice in Wonderland*, with its references to pills, mushrooms, and dream-like experiences. Grace Slick, the band's leader singer, was the queen of the psychedelic sound, her indomitable vibrato vocals swooping and soaring together with Paul Kantner's perfect harmonies riding above the thundering bass of Jack Cassady and the screaming lead guitar of Jorma Koukonen.

The Blues Go Psychedelic

The folk-inspired psychedelic music played by groups like the Grateful Dead and Jefferson Airplane was but one part of the San Francisco sound. Other performers harkened back to rock and roll's blues roots. Singer Janis Joplin was strongly influenced by female blues singer Odetta and blues heavyweight Leadbelly.

After joining a band called Big Brother and the Holding Company in 1966, Joplin became a star almost instantly, drawing heavily from the blues heritage of rock and roll. Joplin was famous for wailing out songs such as "Piece of My Heart" and "Ball and Chain" with eyes closed, face contorted, clutching a microphone in one hand and a bottle of Southern Comfort whiskey in the other. She shrieked, moaned, cried, screamed, and pounded her feet, lost in a world of her own as she sang for thousands of people. Joplin's music could not exactly be called blues, nor was it acid rock; hers was a sound she jokingly called "alkydelic."[24] Joplin's blues came from her sad, lonely soul, and she barely lived to see the end of the sixties, dying of a heroin overdose on October 4, 1970, at the age of twenty-seven, only four years into a meteoric musical career.

Jimi Hendrix's Fuzz-Induced Frenzy

While Janis Joplin was influenced by the gruff and growling vocal styles of blues singers, psychedelic rock pioneer Jimi Hendrix took inspiration from the soulful riffs played by blues guitar players. Hendrix, born in Seattle, Washington, in 1942, has often been labeled by critics as the greatest guitarist of the twentieth century, and few dispute that claim. He began his career backing blues and soul superstars such as Little Richard, Tina Turner, and Wilson Pickett.

In the mid-sixties, Hendrix moved to England, where he put together a trio, the Jimi Hendrix Experience, with drummer Mitch Mitchell and bassist Noel Redding. In live performances, the left-handed Hendrix played his Stratocaster guitar upside down, and was able to create unearthly sounds that humbled established rock guitar slingers such as Peter Townshend of the Who and Eric Clapton of Cream.

Hendrix was unknown in America until 1967, when he played at the Monterey Pop Festival in Monterey, California. Dressed in buckles, beads, and feather boas, Hendrix stood in front of the mesmerized crowd playing guitar with his teeth. The wall of Marshall amplifiers behind him shrieked with feedback as he put his fuzz tone, wah-wah, and phase-effect pedals to the test. As the entire stage groaned and vibrated with the cascade of Hendrix's lead notes during

Jimi Hendrix is considered by many to be the greatest guitarist of the twentieth century.

"Wild Thing," the guitarist bent over, soaked his beloved guitar in lighter fluid, and lit it on fire. By the time the movie chronicling that performance, *Monterey Pop*, was released later that year, Jimi Hendrix was a guitar superstar, and anyone who heard him knew that rock and roll would never be the same.

Hendrix released an incredible three albums in two years: *Are You Experienced?*, *Axis-Bold as Love*, and the double-album *Electric Ladyland*. Songs such as "Purple Haze," "And the Wind Cried Mary," "Little Wing," and his version of the

Bob Dylan song "All Along the Watchtower" became instant radio staples.

In September 1970, it all came crashing down after Hendrix accidentally took too many powerful sleeping pills and mixed them with alcohol. He died just two months short of his twenty-eighth birthday. Although Hendrix's career was cut short, the fuzz-induced frenzy of his guitar work was imitated by a million guitar players, and a new genre—heavy metal—grew up directly from his flying fingers. He changed what it meant to be a lead guitarist, and though many would try, few would have the talent or free spirit to match Hendrix's technical or creative virtuosity.

Counterculture Goes Mainstream

One of the most celebrated moments of Jimi Hendrix's career took place in August 1969, when he played a screaming, psychedelic version of the "The Star Spangled Banner" at the Woodstock Music and Art Fair. Hendrix was the final act at the three-day concert, now known simply as Woodstock. The event took place during the height of the counterculture revolution, and almost half a million people gathered in a field near Bethel, New York, to hear twenty-seven popular musical acts such as the Grateful Dead, Janis Joplin, the Who, Jefferson Airplane, and Crosby, Stills, Nash & Young.

Although Woodstock promoters originally hoped that fifty thousand people would attend, no one was prepared for the teeming throngs that made their way to Woodstock. There was not enough food, water, or bathrooms for the huge crowds and severe rainstorms turned the concert site into a mud pit. Despite the hardships, there was little in the way of violence or crime. As the promoters boasted, with kids running the show, it was simply three days of peace, love, and music.

The youthful organizers of Woodstock might have seen the show's success in such idealistic terms, but record executives saw gold in those New York hills. The music business had grown steadily throughout the sixties, thanks to many of the performers featured at Woodstock, but it seemed that the record companies had underestimated the mass attraction of rock-and-roll music.

As dreamy memories of Woodstock faded away, many record company executives and musicians took a sharp turn away from the idealistic and moved rapidly towards the capitalistic, asking themselves why they were fighting a system that could reward them so well. This contradiction is explored by Ken Tucker in *Rock of Ages: The Rolling Stone History of Rock*:

> In the previous decade, rock was the stuff of the counterculture; in the 1970s . . . this music was the culture. For some longtime rock fans, this was proof positive that rock was no longer any good, that it had sold out and become family entertainment. . . . For others, though, it suggested the enormous outreach and ambition of the music. For the first time in its history, large numbers of people began to think that maybe rock and roll really was here to stay; that it could grow and become an artistic medium that could adapt to its aging audience as well as continue to attract the young fans who would remain the lifeblood of the music. What some saw as the death of rock as a challenging, creative medium, others recognized as an opportunity to spread the music's diverse messages to an unprecedented number of people. And, in some cases, to get rich while doing it.[25]

The Woodstock Effect

One of the first groups to benefit from this new view of rock and roll was Crosby, Stills, Nash & Young (CSN&Y). When CSN&Y performed at Woodstock, it was their first gig, and they were terrified. The band's heartwarming performance was captured for the movie *Woodstock*, released later that year, and the film helped make the band's first album, *Crosby, Stills & Nash* (made without Young), an instant best seller. Although the group's sound was a sort of psychedelic folk music and seemingly unlikely to engender Beatlemania-like hysteria, its star status allowed CS&N to pack large sports stadiums throughout the seventies. Such a

Music as Product

During the early 1970s the record business began a steady expansion, growing at an unprecedented rate of 25 percent a year. This growth attracted the interest of multinational corporations, which purchased the record companies but had little interest in the high ideals of musicians—or in rock and roll as an art form. In the new corporate culture, music became known as product. Songs were something to be labeled, put in a package, and sold as quickly as possible, like a bar of soap or bottle of soda.

The new attitude changed the way songs were promoted. Record executives realized they could reach more consumers if they divided up the music into neat categories and marketed it to specific "demographic" groups, such as older baby boomers, suburban teenagers, or college students. Radio programmers used polls, surveys, and focus groups to determine the type of music their listeners most wanted to hear. What they found in the post-Beatles era was that listeners preferred music that was not available on short-playing singles. This led to the development of a new radio format known as album-oriented rock (AOR), in which songs from albums were played in heavy rotation. AOR became the dominant form of music on FM radio in the following decades.

feat was previously reserved for huge bands like the Beatles and Rolling Stones.

Crosby, Stills & Nash made history in another way, too. When their 1970 album, *Déjà Vu*, sold several million copies upon release, it established a standard by which record sales would be measured from then on. In the fifties and sixties, a gold record—an album that sold at least a half a million copies—was considered a huge success. After Woodstock, the threshold was raised dramatically, and popular records were expected to go platinum, selling a million copies, or multiplatinum, with several million copies sold.

Dark Side of the Moon

Crosby, Stills & Nash and other post-Woodstock bands followed a trend that began with the Beatles' album *Sgt. Pepper*. Rather than writing hit singles, post-Woodstock superstars like CS&N and Santana created entire albums on which every song was a potential hit. This led to the growth of album-oriented radio (AOR) programming in the early 1970s. AOR originated when DJs began playing "deep cuts," or songs from albums that record companies never promoted as hit singles. This occurred during an era when the number of FM music stations exploded and the overall quality of FM, which could broadcast in stereo, greatly enhanced the listening experience. The main beneficiaries of

The original members of Pink Floyd were a well known underground psychedelic band in Cambridge, England.

this trend were English rock bands like Pink Floyd and Led Zeppelin, who became AOR staples in the 1970s.

Pink Floyd started out in 1966 playing psychedelic music in the college town of Cambridge, England, at "underground" parties where art students were dropping acid. Although they were well-known in England, their quirky, late-sixties psychedelic albums like *Ummagumma*, *Atom Heart Mother*, and *Meddle* only sold moderately well in the United States.

Pink Floyd's underground status quickly changed in 1973, though, with the release of its eighth album, *The Dark Side of the Moon*. The album's theme was gloomy: The songs were about Pink Floyd founding member Syd Barrett's descent into madness. But the sonic pictures painted by the group struck a chord with the masses. As Pink Floyd guitarist Dave Gilmour later commented: "The words were brilliant, it had a lovely cover, and . . . [there] was something to appeal to everyone in the world in at least one of the songs, and everything gelled perfectly at that one moment."[26] *The Dark Side of the Moon* sold 45 million copies and remained on *Billboard*'s Top LP charts a record-setting 741 weeks (more than fourteen years), from 1973 to 1988.

Pink Floyd toured relentlessly throughout the seventies, their stage shows growing in size and extravagance. In an era of rock excess, Pink Floyd went beyond all bounds, constructing a huge wall onstage during performances of songs from the album *The Wall*. The group disbanded in 1983, but it is one of the most successful bands of the era. They sold more than 200 million albums, and their generation-spanning music remains popular today.

Heavy Metal Monsters of Rock

While Pink Floyd was known for its onstage extravagance, heavy metal heroes Led Zeppelin were famous for their off-stage excesses, which often involved massive quantities of drugs and dozens of female fans known as groupies. Formed in Great Britain in 1969, Led Zeppelin took the heavy blues music of Howlin' Wolf and Willie Dixon and rewrote it for a new era. The group also fused the blues with folklore and

The Doors' Revolt, Disorder, and Chaos

Sixties rock and roll was revolutionary music, and few musicians upset the social order with more relish than Jim Morrison, lead singer for the Doors. Morrison was fascinated with fire, surrealistic experiences, and exploring the depths of human consciousness. These themes were explored in songs such as "Light My Fire," "Strange Days," "Moonlight Drive," and "Break on Through."

With his tight leather pants, mop of wavy hair, and movie-idol good looks, Morrison was the prototypical bad-boy rock star. He appeared onstage violently drunk while alternately insulting audiences and inciting them to riot and revolt. Morrison gave reasons for his rowdy behavior in his official biography for Elektra Records in 1966:

> I've always been attracted to ideas that were about revolt against authority. I like ideas about the breaking away or overthrowing of established order. I am interested in anything about revolt, disorder, chaos—especially activity that seems to have no meaning. It seems to me to be the road toward freedom—external revolt is a way to bring about internal freedom.

Morrison died in 1971, little more than half a year after Jimi Hendrix and Janis Joplin. Although the music of the Doors retains a fundamental grip on the playlists of modern radio stations, the group represented a wild, free, and often frightening aspect of a decade of protest and youth revolution.

Quoted in Bill Hadley, "Bios." Doors History, 2010. www.doorshistory.com/bios.

Celtic mythology, producing AOR staples such as "Stairway to Heaven."

Led Zeppelin's sound was driven by Jimmy Page's unholy fuzz-saturated staccato guitar riffs, John Paul Jones's bass barrage, John Bonham's arena-shattering drums, and

Robert Plant's shrieking vocals. Their blues-based heavy metal was worshipped by fans everywhere, and by the time they released the album *Led Zeppelin III* in October 1970, the band was the top rock act in the world.

Jimmy Page was fascinated by the occult, and rumors spread that Led Zeppelin practiced black magic. When the group's instant success inspired an army of heavy metal

The Who

The music of the Who was some of the most original of the early 1970s, and their antics during live performances often shocked audiences. Onstage, the group performed their original songs such as "Magic Bus," "My Generation," and "Baba O'Riley" with a punk attitude as singer Roger Daltrey swung his microphone on its long wire in wide arcs, drummer Keith Moon savagely pounded his drum kit, and guitarist Pete Townshend leapt in the air and strummed his guitar with a stiff-armed windmill motion that invented the concept of playing "air guitar" among fans. At the end of the evening, Moon kicked over his drums as Townshend rammed his guitar into the shredded speakers of his amplifier. Meanwhile, bassist John Entwistle stood almost comically stoic, holding down the rhythm in the midst of chaos. With multiplatinum albums like *Tommy*, *Who's Next*, and *Who Are You*, the Who had sold more than 100 million records by 2011.

Pete Townshend leaps across the stage at Live Aid in London in 1985. These and other antics of The Who shocked fans during live performances in the 1970s.

bands, the occult became linked with the music style, especially with bands like Black Sabbath. These early heavy metal bands spawned a massive group of imitators that included Metallica, Megadeth, and AC/DC. Each tried to outdo each other in outrageous behavior on and offstage.

Ziggy Plays Guitar

The excesses of bands like Led Zeppelin contributed to their reputation for testing boundaries, and Led Zeppelin's appearance enhanced that aura. Jimmy Page and Robert Plant pranced around the stage with tight pants, frilly shirts, and

David Bowie invented the genre of glitter rock. He is seen here performing as his alter ego Ziggy Stardust in London in 1973.

long curls, feminizing the image of rock stars. As the lines between male and female rock fashion began to blur in the early 1970s, singer David Bowie dropped into the middle of the scene portraying an androgynous spaceman on a mission.

Bowie, born David Jones in London in 1947, became an "overnight sensation" in 1972 with the release of *The Rise and Fall of Ziggy Stardust and the Spiders from Mars*. For the album, Bowie assumed the personality of a fictional character, Ziggy Stardust, who was supposed to be the biggest rock star in the world—one who came from outer space. In concert, Bowie appeared in white face paint with his hair dyed carrot-orange. He dressed in red knee-high platform boots and a brightly colored, skin-tight jumpsuit. In the process, Bowie became a rock star of unearthly proportions.

With this act, Bowie almost single-handedly invented the genre known as theatrical rock, or glitter or glam rock (for his glamorous fashion statements). In this style of rock, the music was almost beside the point. Bowie commented on his invention in 1972: "My performances have got to be theatrical experiences for me as well as the audience. . . . I think it should be tarted up, made into a prostitute, a parody of itself. . . . I should be the clown. . . . The music is the mask the message wears . . . and I, the performer, am the message."[27]

In 1974 Bowie abandoned his spaceman outfits in favor of stylish white suits. But once the glam rock genie was out of the bottle, it could not be contained. Singers such as Alice Cooper reveled in rock-and-roll theatrics. It was not unusual to see Cooper onstage in bizarre makeup, with a giant boa constrictor wrapped around his neck, or involved in a mock execution on a neck-chopping guillotine. The rock group Kiss took glam rock one step further. After rising to fame in 1975, members of Kiss never appeared in public without full face paint and outrageous costumes.

Just as the face of American culture had changed since the mid-sixties, so too did the image of rock-and-roll stars. The notes played and the words written during that era transformed the world, and they would continue to influence rock musicians well into the twenty-first century.

CHAPTER 4

The Psychotic World of Punk

In the mid-1970s rock music was divided and carved up by entertainment industry executives who wished to market a variety of sounds to different age groups, races, and regions. As a result, rock fans were presented with a variety of new styles. As rock critic Steve Pond explains, this created a problem:

> Rock had no center. . . . [There] was no unifying presence in rock [like the Beatles]. . . . So rock in the Seventies quickly became diffuse[d], scattered and unfocused, fragmenting into little genres . . . [with] a hundred different focal points: Elton John for popsters; Led Zeppelin for hard rockers; Joni Mitchell for the singer/songwriter contingent; David Bowie for glam-rockers; Stevie Wonder for soul aficionados. Instead of a center, rock had a bunch of radio formats.[28]

The format that dominated throughout the late 1970s and early '80s was album-oriented radio. In an era before digital downloads and Internet music stores like iTunes, most rock fans heard their music on FM radio and on their home music systems. If a band was popular on AOR, they could expect to sell millions of records. Since many FM radio stations had been purchased by huge entertainment corporations, their playlists became increasingly conservative. The major record companies shied away from rock music that was rebellious, challenging, and dangerous and promoted music that was, in Pond's words, "slick, sleek and, as often as not, soulless."[29] The ultimate expression of this trend was heard in the predictable synthesizer licks and drum machine beats of disco songs. Between 1976 and 1980, disco acts like Gloria Gaynor, Donna Summer, Patti LaBelle, and KC and the Sunshine Band were amazingly popular, dominating the *Billboard* record sales charts.

Progressive Rock

Besides disco, most of the popular music in the second half of the seventies was recorded by progressive rock bands like Rush, Styx, and REO Speedwagon. These groups pushed the boundaries of rock and roll by incorporating complex elements of jazz and symphonic classical music into their songs. Progressive rock bands like Yes melded instrumental wizardry with lyrics that evoked images from science fiction and fantasy novels.

While most progressive groups lacked the sheer talent—and popularity—of the Beatles, they had advantages not available to sixties recording groups. Whereas the Beatles recorded *Sgt. Pepper* using only four-track tape, seventies bands had access to twenty-four- and thirty-two-track recording technology. Larry Starr, a professor of music, and Christopher Waterman, a professor of arts and culture, explain how this technology changed the sound of music:

> [The advent of] 32-track recording consoles and electronic sound devices allowed musicians . . . to create complex aural textures, and to construct a given track on an LP over a period of time, adding and subtracting (or "punching in" and "punching out") individual instruments and voices. . . . Some rock bands became famous for spending many months (and tons of money) in the studio to create a single rock "masterpiece."[30]

Progressive rockers Steely Dan and the country rock group the Eagles were among the many bands of the era known to spend countless hours in the studio. The Eagles' album *Hotel California* took eighteen months to record (by way of comparison, the Beatles' *Sgt. Pepper* took four months). The work paid off, however, as *Hotel California* became one of the best-selling albums in history.

The Roots of Punk

The well-publicized indulgence of rock superstars occurred during an era when average Americans were confronted with high unemployment, price inflation, and gasoline shortages. During the second half of the 1970s, millions of workers lost their jobs when steel mills and auto assembly lines shut down. Unemployment rose to levels not seen since

Disco

In the second half of the 1970s, disco music conquered the radio airwaves and then crashed as rapidly as it had ascended. Disco is dance music that melds sixties soul, Latin music, and funk. The style features a prominent bass line, an "electro" synthesizer sound, and an insistent syncopated drumbeat usually provided by a drum machine. Disco music originated in big-city dance clubs where African American, Hispanic, and gay dancers congregated. The style was invented by disc jockeys who used turntables to spin short song sequences to create dance music with fast, loud, beat-heavy crescendos. Disco became a record industry phenomenon in 1976, when acts like Donna Summer, Gloria Gaynor, Patti LaBelle, and KC and the Sunshine Band rose to the top of the pop charts. In 1977 the film *Saturday Night Fever* and its top-selling sound track brought disco to mainstream America.

Disco's downfall occurred around 1980, when rock fans began reacting violently to the music. Disco records were burned during radio station promotional events and T-shirts emblazoned with "Disco Sucks" became an emblem of the era. Disco was dead by 1981, but the infectious beat became ubiquitous in rock songs made by everyone from the Rolling Stones and Madonna to the Grateful Dead.

Although they were not well known outside of the New York art scene The Velvet Underground became one of the most influential pre-punk bands.

the Great Depression of the 1930s. Some of America's biggest cities—including Cleveland, Ohio; Detroit, Michigan; and New York, New York—faced bankruptcy and were left without enough money to fix roads, repair schools, or place enough police on the streets to keep order.

The situation was worse in England, where power outages, strikes by garbage workers, and frighteningly high unemployment gripped the nation. For many teenagers growing up during this time, progressive rock music did not address their concerns, and the sixties-era ideals of peace and love seemed like a joke. The anger and hopelessness that grew in place of that idealism fueled a new kind of music known as punk rock.

While punk rock gained momentum in the seventies,

the founding members of the movement were in the Velvet Underground, a band that was formed in 1965 by singer/songwriter Lou Reed, drummer Maureen Tucker, guitarist Sterling Morrison, and pianist/bassist/violist John Cale. As millions of Americans were dropping acid, growing long hair, and dressing like hippies, Reed tested the boundaries even more, writing songs about forbidden topics such as homosexuality, bisexuality, heroin addiction, transvestism, and death. His off-key, flat-toned, droll vocals were backed by a sonic assault from the band that combined free-form jazz improvisation with two-chord rock, rhythm and blues, and avant-garde experimentation.

The Velvet Underground was strongly influenced by the art movement known as minimalism, in which artists used basic colors and geometric shapes to produce uncluttered abstract paintings and sculptures. In music, minimalism meant the use of simple rhythms and tones and repeated or sustained melodies that sometimes resulted in a hypnotic effect.

Few people outside the New York artist underground were ready for the band's combination of twisted love songs, white noise, and celebration of heroin. While the Velvet Underground failed to reach the charts, its 1968 album *White Light/White Heat* would become one of the most influential pre-punk, or proto-punk, albums in history. *White Light/White Heat* is full of simple two- or three-chord songs. On it, Reed spits, yells, and recites vocals in an almost rap-like dirge, while guitars wail and screech feedback in the mix. Raw, emotional, and musically unprofessional, this second and final album from the Velvet Underground inspired Detroit punk icons Iggy Pop and the Stooges in the late sixties and nearly every other punk rocker who followed in their wake.

CBGB & OMFUG

By the mid-seventies the center of the punk movement could be found in a New York City nightclub called CBGB, located on the run-down Bowery on Manhattan's Lower East Side. During this era, the neighborhood was full of

Detroit Kicks Out the Jams

In the late 1960s, hard-rock, proto-punk anger was sweeping across the industrial Midwest. That blind rage found its voice in MC5, a rock band combining pounding heavy metal power chords, feedback, fuzzy grunge guitar, and a relentless rhythm section that could make listeners' ears ring. Based in Detroit, a tough city mired in crime, urban riots, and industrial decay, MC5 produced songs that preached the radical politics of anarchy and revolution. Their most famous song, "Kick Out the Jams," began with an obscenity that few middle-class record buyers used at that time.

The only artist who could be said to compete with MC5 was Iggy Pop, born James Newell Osterberg near Ann Arbor, Michigan, in 1947. Inspired by the Velvet Underground, Pop founded the Stooges in 1967 and experimented with making music on oil drums, vacuum cleaners, and other objects. While singing about isolation, discontentment, and sexual aggression over crunchy guitar rhythms, Pop slithered around onstage like a snake, pouring beer over his head, spitting it at the audience and, sometimes, cutting his chest and arms with broken beer bottles. Pop's music, along with that of the MC5 underground, provided the sonic foundation for the punk movement that would follow.

abandoned buildings where winos, homeless drug addicts, dealers, and hookers spent their days.

CBGB opened in 1973. Its full name, CBGB & OMFUG, was an acronym for the music that was supposed to grace its stages: Country, Bluegrass, Blues, and Other Music for Uplifting Gormandizers. (A gormandizer is someone who eats greedily—a glutton—but in this case, it was meant to denote people who enthusiastically consumed music.) Although few country or bluegrass bands ever played at the club, CBGB quickly attracted an underground rock scene made up of bands that played original music but lacked the connections that would allow them to play at more established Manhattan nightclubs, which only booked bands that had major-label recording contracts. The owner of CBGB only hired bands that had nowhere else to play.

The neighborhood surrounding CBGB had apartments with cheap rent, which attracted struggling artists, actors, writers, poets, and musicians. These people composed an instant fan base for the experimental bands that played at CBGB, such as Television, whose leader, Richard Hell, modeled the group's free-jazz–style jams after the Velvet Underground.

Hell is credited with inventing the punk fashion aesthetic by wearing short, spiky hair and ripped-up T-shirts held together with safety pins. Future Sex Pistols' manager Malcolm McLaren describes Hell: "Here was a guy all deconstructed, torn down, looking like he just crawled out of a drain hole, looking like he was covered in slime, looking like he hadn't slept in years, looking like he hadn't washed in years."[31] Hell summed up his apathetic punk attitude with his song "(I Belong to) The Blank Generation," which became an anthem for those in the early punk movement.

Patti Smith's Punk Poetry

Patti Smith was one of the disaffected neighborhood poets drawn to CBGB. Smith had been reading her poetry in New York coffeehouses since 1970, and in 1974 she began reciting her poems backed by the guitar of Lenny Kaye. By 1975 Smith and Kaye had formed a band and were a regular attraction at CBGB. Smith's songs gained notice from Arista Records, and she was the first punk rocker to land a major recording contract.

Smith's first album, *Horses*, was released to wide critical acclaim. The album contains songs that feature her reedy voice singing and reciting her imaginative poetry over sparse musical arrangements. Smith also included a few punked-up rock classics such as "Land of a Thousand Dances," a sixties hit for soul artist Wilson Pickett, and "Gloria," by the Irish rocker Van Morrison.

Smith's successive albums further cemented her reputation as a talented poet and punk music innovator. In 1978

Patti Smith and her band at the final concert before the closing of the iconic New York club CBGB.

she teamed up with Bruce Springsteen to write "Because the Night," which catapulted her into the annals of rock stardom. Throughout her long career, Smith came to be considered a Bob Dylan-like poet of punk, and her original sound and unbridled musical emotion would be emulated by scores of artists during the years following her success.

The Ramones: Power Punk

In February 1976, a few months after Patti Smith released *Horses*, the Ramones became the second punk rock band to produce a record on a major label. The Ramones was a group of unrelated guys who all changed their last name to Ramone—Joey Ramone, Dee Dee Ramone, Marky Ramone, and Tommy Ramone. The Ramones played their first gig at CBGB in 1974, and quickly became a featured act at the club. They dressed in tight jeans and black leather jackets and wore moptop Beatles hairdos. Although their look was hardly original, the Ramones stripped all pretension from

The Revolutionary Spirit of Rock and Roll

In her award-winning 2010 autobiography, Just Kids, punk rock pioneer Patti Smith describes her band's musical philosophy:

We imagined ourselves as the [eighteenth-century American patriot group] Sons of Liberty with a mission to preserve, protect, and project the revolutionary spirit of rock and roll. We feared that the music which had given us sustenance was in danger of spiritual starvation. We feared it losing its sense of purpose, we feared it falling into fattened hands, we feared it floundering in a mire of spectacle, finance, and vapid technical complexity. We would call forth in our minds the image of Paul Revere, riding through the American night, petitioning the people to wake up, to take up arms. We too would take up arms, the arms of our generation, the electric guitar and the microphone.

Patti Smith. *Just Kids*. New York: HarperCollins, 2010, p. 180.

rock music. Their two-chord power punk songs sounded like psycho surfer music played by a demented Buddy Holly. Drummer Tommy Ramone describes the band's music: "We took the rock sound into a psychotic world and narrowed it down into a straight line of energy. In an era of progressive rock, with its complexities and counterpoints, we had a perspective of non-musicality and intelligence that took over from musicianship."[32]

The Ramones played fast and loud. With no one in the group competent enough to take solos, their sound consisted of a brick wall of earsplitting guitar chords hurled at the audience. Most of their songs clocked in at under two minutes, and their entire set lasted less than twenty. In a 1975 review, cultural critic James Wolcott wrote that the Ramones "play with a chopping [frenzy], the pace so brutal that the audience can barely catch its breath. A Ramones rampage is intoxicating—it's exciting to hear their voltage sizzle."[33]

The Ramones' self-titled debut album contained the

The Ramones, despite creating now-classic punk anthems, had most of their success outside of the United States.

now-classic punk anthems "Blitzkrieg Bop," "Beat on the Brat," "Judy Is a Punk," and "Chain Saw," but it only reached number 111 on the *Billboard* charts. The music of the Ramones proved to be much more popular overseas. When they toured Great Britain during the summer of 1976, disaffected English teenagers heard beauty in their music. The group's second album, *Leave Home*, barely registered on the charts in the United States in 1977, but hit number forty-eight in England. With catchy sing-along anthems such as "Pinhead," "Gimme Gimme Shock Treatment," and "Suzy Is a Headbanger," the Ramones planted the roots of punk in England, which soon created pandemonium on both sides of the Atlantic.

Johnny Rotten Hates Pink Floyd

During the summer of 1975, even before the Ramones had toured England, a British shopkeeper named Malcolm McLaren attended the CBGB rock festival, which featured forty bands that had no recording contracts. McLaren was not there to hear the music; he was looking for new and strange fashions to sell in his clothing store. He also tried to convince Richard Hell to move to England to front a band of McLaren's creation. Hell refused, as British rock critic Pete Fame writes, "so McLaren borrowed his image."[34]

Although not a musician himself, McLaren saw an opportunity to make money from punk rock music. To attract attention, he named his London shop Sex and stocked it with punk fashions. Like CBGB, McLaren's store quickly became a magnet for artists, bored, angry teenagers, and rock-and-roll hopefuls. Among them were guitarist Steve Jones and drummer Paul Cook, who had been playing the music of Iggy Pop and the Stooges since 1972. McLaren paired the two with bassist Glen Matlock, who worked behind the counter in the shop, and the band began looking for a lead singer who was shocking enough to gain the group some publicity. McLaren seized on an angry, acne-faced store regular named John Lydon.

Lydon was a green-haired nineteen-year-old who wore a homemade shirt with the scrawled message "I Hate Pink Floyd." When asked to audition for the band, Lydon grabbed an old showerhead for a microphone and shrieked his way through the Alice Cooper song "Eighteen" while it played on the store jukebox. Because of the foul condition of his decaying teeth, Jones dubbed the singer Johnny Rotten. It was obvious to all that Rotten could not sing, but he was hired because he had written a few pages of song lyrics and, as Jones recalls, "Rotten looked the part, with the green hair. . . . Then again, we couldn't play [either] so it was okay."[35]

McLaren decided to call his new band the Sex Pistols after seeing the slogan on a T-shirt in his shop. Adding Rotten to the band would prove to be a canny move. Rotten wrote songs about anarchy, violence, fascism, and apathy. Onstage, he taunted the audience, screamed insults, spit beer, and threw himself about, bouncing off amps and drums like a rag doll. In a 2000 documentary about the Sex Pistols titled *The Filth and the Fury*, Rotten describes his stage attitude: "We [wanted] to offend all the people we were fed up with.

We went into full attack format. This band wasn't about making people happy, it was about attack. Attack, attack, attack."[36]

Anarchy in the United Kingdom

The Sex Pistols signed with EMI in 1976 and released their first single, "Anarchy in the UK." In the song, Rotten screams that he is an anarchist and the Antichrist. When band members appeared extremely drunk on an early evening live television talk show to promote the song, they unloaded a stream of foul language that shocked the audience. The next day EMI dropped the band. In the interim, the group decided that bassist Matlock was far too clean-cut for the band's raunchy image. He was fired and replaced by Sid Vicious, who, although he was unable to play bass, was the perfect foil for Rotten. Vicious lived up to his name, gouging himself with beer bottles and cracking heads in the audience with his heavy Fender bass guitar.

In March 1977 the band released "God Save the Queen." This song, which savaged the revered Queen Elizabeth, created even more controversy in a nation where insulting the queen was tantamount to burning the flag. Worse, the record sleeve depicted the queen's face with a safety pin through her nose. Although the song was banned by British radio stations, it soared to number one in sales.

The band released the album *Never Mind the Bollocks—Here's the Sex Pistols* in 1977 and played a tour of the United States the following year. By this time Vicious was a heroin addict; he was often so high that he was barely able to stand up onstage. Vicious died of a heroin overdose in February of 1979, a year after the Sex Pistols disbanded.

Although the Sex Pistols only lasted a little more than two years. they changed the 1970s rock-and-roll ethos with their outrageous performances and anti-authoritarian music. The group exhibited the ultimate expression of the punk attitude that embraced raw emotion, unflinching social commentary, and basic three-chord rock and roll. Along with the Ramones, Patti Smith, and Television, the Sex Pistols rescued rock and roll during a decade of pretentiousness and went on to influence hundreds of bands in later decades, including Nirvana and Green Day.

Punk's New Wave

By 1980 it was obvious that punk music would never find a large audience despite near-universal praise from rock critics on both sides of the Atlantic. As punk crashed and burned, the fast, crude, angry music was supplanted by a second wave, or new wave, of bands that fused punk rock beats with a smart, arty, ironic, and cool attitude. This new ethos was popularized by the band Blondie and was epitomized by the group the Talking Heads.

Singer-songwriter-guitarist David Byrne formed the Talking Heads in 1974 after meeting drummer Chris Frantz and bassist Tina Weymouth at the fine arts college the Rhode Island School of Design (RISD). The trio was soon joined by keyboardist and guitarist Jerry Harrison. The Talking Heads began appearing as an opening act for the Ramones at CBGB in 1975.

The Talking Heads were a successful part of the new wave movement of the late 1970s, producing multiple gold and platinum records.

The Talking Heads were signed by Sire Records in 1977 and in the years that followed, the group released a string of gold and platinum albums including *More Songs About Buildings and Food*, *Fear of Music*, and *Remain in Light*. The 1983 album *Speaking in Tongues* produced the band's biggest hit, "Burning Down the House." In 1984 the Talking Heads released the live concert film *Stop Making Sense*, in which Byrne appears in a comical oversize suit that gives him the appearance of a lost, shrinking man. His stage persona is described by Larry Starr and Christopher Waterman: "Byrne often delivered his lyrics in a nervous, almost schizophrenic stream-of-consciousness voice, like overheard fragments from a psychiatrist's office."[37] Byrne's alienated weirdness stood in stark contrast to the music. The Talking Heads laid down tight funk grooves with interlocking bass and drum grooves and catchy gospel-like choruses, all punctuated by hot guitar licks and ticklish synthesizer thrusts.

Punk Goes Hard Core

While new-wave music found broad acceptance in mainstream America, seventies punk spawned another style. Hard-core punk made the Sex Pistols seem almost tame by comparison. Hard core was created and championed by the children of baby boomers. This demographic was inadvertently dubbed by the mainstream media with the punk-sounding name Generation X.

Members of Gen X had completely different perspectives and expectations than those of the post–World War II generation. Gen Xers grew up in an era of high divorce rates, AIDS, gang violence, and destructive drugs such as crack. In addition, three recessions in the United States during the 1980s and early '90s created unemployment that left many young people with diminished economic prospects. The music of the era reflected their anger and disaffection. As the founder of Sub Pop records Jonathan Poneman stated: "[When you] see a lot of [your] dreams subside because of this particularly brutal recession, and class warfare, race warfare, it makes you very angry, very fearful, very

Blondie's Heart of Glass

Blondie was one of the most popular new-wave bands in the world during the second half of the 1970s. The group was formed in 1974 by guitarist Chris Stein and singer/songwriter Deborah Harry. Drummer Clem Burke and keyboard player Jimmy Destri joined the following year. After playing New York cult club CBGB for a few years, Blondie attained mainstream success in 1978 with the release of their third album *Parallel Lines*, which contained the hit single "Heart of Glass." The music on *Parallel Lines* was heavily influenced by 1960s girl group tunes, surf music, and disco. Harry's lyrics were ironic, humorous, and often mocking. Her image as a glamorous platinum-blond movie star helped make her an international celebrity.

Blondie combined high-energy pop, rock, punk, reggae, and funk on the 1979 album *Eat to the Beat*. To promote the album, the band created music videos for each song, and sold them on VHS tape. This was several years before MTV went on the air. In 1980 Blondie broke new ground once again with the number-one hit "Rapture," which has Harry rapping the lyrics. "Rapture" was the first rap song to top the singles charts and contained the first rap music most white Americans had ever heard.

Debbie Harry of Blondie, seen here performing in Central Park in 1979, used her platinum blonde movie star image to become an international celebrity.

alienated. And those are qualities that lead to an unusually rebellious passionate rock."[38]

Lyrics to hard-core punk songs were aimed at desperate and alienated American youth. The music was played as loudly as possible and accompanied by whatever stage antics generated the most shock. Hard-core performers might appear onstage wielding chainsaws and dressed in vinyl, plastic, black leather—or nothing at all.

Following in the footsteps of Johnny Rotten and Sid Vicious, hard-core musicians adopted nicknames like Don Bonebreak, Darby Crash, and Pat Smear. Band names such as X, Germ, Bad Religion, and Black Flag (named after a popular household insecticide) spoke volumes about the music the groups performed. Song titles, too, reflected the attitude of the music. Black Flag's set lists included searing titles such as "Depression," "Revenge," "Dead Inside," and "Life of Pain." Henry Rollins, who wrote the songs, describes his motivation: "Pain is my girlfriend; that's how I see it. I feel pain every day of my life. When you see me perform, it's that pain you're seeing coming out. I put all my emotions, all my feelings, and my body on the line. People hurt me. I hurt myself—mentally, physically."[39]

Since record companies refused to touch bands like Black Flag, hard-core groups started their own independent record labels to distribute their music. Some, like Bad Religion, were quite successful. After its members started Epitaph Records in 1980, they sold 7 million copies of their album *Smash*.

The hard-core scene that began in Los Angeles, California, spread to other cities throughout the United States. In the early 1980s Minneapolis, Minnesota, bands such as Hüsker Dü and the Replacements melded heavy metal power chords with punk and hard core. During the same era, San Francisco's Dead Kennedys, led by singer Jello Biafra, mixed hard-core music with ironic left-wing social commentary in songs such as "Kill the Poor" and "Lynch the Landlord."

The attitude of hard-core punk was that anybody could play the music, and the walls between audience and performer were broken down. This led to a new form of violent physical expression seen in front of stages when hard-core bands performed. As Biafra states, "[When] younger people [started] coming to our shows in droves, they brought the arena rock mentality with them, including fights [and] jumping off the stage just to see if you could hit people."[40] This led to audience members slamming into each other, or "moshing," while dancing.

Nearly every generation rebels against the one before it, and Johnny Rotten, Sid Vicious, Jello Biafra, and Pat Smear were about as different from John, Paul, George, and Ringo as they could possibly be.

CHAPTER 5

From Pop Rock to the Heaviest Metal

In 1982 several prominent critics wrote obituaries for rock and roll. Robert Christgau, the music and cultural commentator for the *Village Voice*, stated: "Teen rebellion and electric guitars aren't looking particularly eternal these days." *Newsweek* music critic Jim Miller concluded, "Rock 'n' roll has a future all right. But whether it can ever recapture its cutting edge and resume a leading role in defining the frontiers of America's popular culture is another matter entirely."[41]

Several developments fueled the laments of the critics. While punk remained popular in Great Britain, the outrageous and angry music had stunningly failed to incite a musical revolution in the United States. Album-oriented radio, which promoted slick, produced pop rock acts like Boston, Foreigner, Fleetwood Mac, and Bob Seger, remained extremely popular among America's teenagers. Another major challenge to cutting-edge rock rebellion could be traced to the introduction of synthesizers and computer-programmed drum machines during the disco era, which changed the sound of rock music. The rough, jangly, distorted electric guitars and slightly off-kilter drums of earlier times were replaced by efficient—and some would say soulless—sounds of electronic-generated beats.

I Want My MTV

Synthesizers and drum machines shaped the sounds of a number of British new-wave bands in the early 1980s, including Culture Club, Duran Duran, and Adam and the Ants. The look and sound of these groups was a reaction to, and rejection of, punk fashions and music. The British groups combined colorful, flamboyant fashions with the danceable sounds of disco, R&B, rock, and electronic pop. The music was labeled new romanticism, synth pop, techno pop, or electro pop.

New romanticism began as an underground movement in England. To attract attention to new romantic music and fashions, bands produced short promotional videos that showed members lip-synching, or mouthing the words to their songs. Typical videos were theatrical and cinematic

Spinal Tap Mocks Heavy Metal

In 1984 comedians Michael McKean, Christopher Guest, and Harry Shearer wrote and starred in *This Is Spinal Tap*, a Grammy-nominated movie that mercilessly ridiculed the new-wave British heavy metal rock scene. Dubbed a "mockumentary" because it was a mock documentary, the movie portrayed the comeback American tour of the fictional has-been band Spinal Tap. With silly long-hair wigs and pasted-on facial hair, Spinal Tap played ridiculous, over-the-top heavy metal songs such as "Smell the Glove," "Gimme Some Money," "Big Bottom," and "Sex Farm" from their album *This Is Spinal Tap*. Band members were utterly clueless as to their politically incorrect behavior, and drummers tended to burst into flames for no reason. With the success of their movie, Spinal Tap continued with the joke for decades, releasing the album *Break Like the Wind* in 1992 and playing concerts on the Back From the Dead tour in 2000. And like all great rock bands, real or imagined, Spinal Tap was featured on an episode of the TV show *The Simpsons*.

with rapidly changing scenes, camera angles sweeping left to right, and zoom shots moving in and out. Jump cuts—very short clips of scenes shot from different angles—were spliced together to add excitement to visuals that often included high-fashion models and musicians with weird haircuts and glittery suits.

New romanticism quickly moved out of the musical underground and into mainstream listening thanks to a historic development in the United States. On August 1, 1981, a new station called Music Television, or MTV, went on the air, backed by a relatively minor $20 million commitment from Warner Cable. Industry critics at first doubted that people would want to "listen" to music on their televisions. but they were quickly proved wrong. By 1983 MTV was seen in 17 million homes. During this era, the station played music videos twenty-four hours a day, seven days a week. Shows were hosted by on-air personalities known as VJs, or video jockeys.

In Great Britain bands had been producing music videos, called song films or promotional clips, since the 1960s. These promotional clips helped sell records when shown on British television programs while the bands were busy touring and could not play live. Because of the popularity of song films in Great Britain, new romantic acts like Billy Idol, Duran Duran, the Thompson Twins, and Flock of Seagulls had TV-ready music videos long before American groups. With its need to play music all day, MTV put their videos in heavy rotation and, in the process, made huge stars of these previously unknown British acts. Robert Christgau was extremely critical of this new trend:

> [Most] rock videos diminish the second-rate songs they're supposed to enhance. . . . Because videos visualize lyrics and compel contemplation of the artists' mugs [faces], they bring home how slick, stunted, smug, self-pitying, and stupid rock culture has become. . . . They replace spectatorism on the physical level as well—fans watch raptly instead of dancing or at least boogieing in the aisles.[42]

Thrilling Video Viewers

The public largely ignored the critical analysis of MTV. The station continued to attract viewers, and even earned the praise of rock critics in later years when it introduced new styles of rock music to the world, like alternative and grunge. For most of the 1980s, however, MTV's greatest success came from promoting pop rockers. The music channel spawned a new generation of stars whose looks and styles received as much attention as their music. Multitalented singer Michael Jackson proved to be perfectly suited to this new medium.

Jackson was a child prodigy who had recorded with his brothers in the hugely popular group the Jackson 5 on the Motown label during the 1970s. When Jackson released his sixth solo album, *Thriller*, in early 1983, the album entered the *Billboard* Top 10 chart at number one. With a variety of musical styles, the album appealed to a wide mainstream audience. *Thriller* contained slick funk disco, hard rock,

Michael Jackson in the "Thriller" video, one of many expensive, elaborate musical mini-movies from the album of the same name.

middle-of-the-road ballads, and sweet soul. In 1987 cultural critic Greg Tate described the album:

> Everything on that record manages a savvy balance between machine language and human intervention, between palpitating [fluttering] heart and precision tuning. *Thriller* is a record that doesn't know how to stop giving pleasure. Every note on the [album] sings and breathes masterful pop instincts: the drumbeats, the bass lines, [and] the guitar chicken scratches.[43]

Jackson's videos for *Thriller* were expensive, theatrical masterpieces, musical mini-movies that received constant airplay on MTV. Jackson showed off his fashion sense and skillful dance moves on "Billie Jean," "Beat It," and "Thriller." This helped *Thriller* remain on the album charts for seventy-eight weeks—thirty-seven weeks at number one. Before the decade was over, *Thriller* sold more than 40 million copies and became the best-selling record in history. At one point the record was selling a million copies a week.

"Where Dance Clubs and Malls Meet"

By featuring the clean-cut Michael Jackson and British "haircut" bands, MTV avoided controversy in the early years. That changed in 1984 when Madonna released her second album *Like a Virgin*, which featured intense dance rock, robotic funk, and soul.

Madonna appeared in videos from *Like a Virgin* as a sultry sex symbol, dancing suggestively in revealing outfits. Her performances generated unwanted attention from conservative family values organizations, which accused the singer of promoting materialism and sex before marriage. Conservative social critic Pam Howar said Madonna was teaching young girls "how to be a porn queen in heat."[44]

As is often the case, controversy helped sell records, and during the Christmas season of 1984, teenage girls lined up outside record stores to purchase *Like a Virgin*. Many fans were already following Madonna's street smart and

Madonna's success helped open doors for women in the mostly male world of rock and roll.

inventive fashion sensibilities. With her arms dripping in bracelets and her funky secondhand-clothing-store fashions, Madonna changed the way young women dressed virtually overnight.

After the success of *Like a Virgin*, Madonna became a movie star and international sensation. In 1990 *LA Weekly* music journalist Danny "Shredder" Weizmann praised Madonna and *Like a Virgin*, describing the album's ongoing cultural influence:

On this album, dedicated to "the virgins of the world," Madonna finds the fifth-dimensional spaces where dance clubs and malls meet. . . . [The song "Like a Virgin"] matches erotic and innocent impulses in a single shot. . . . [Back] in 1984 the lusty positivity of songs like "Dress You Up" was so forward it was almost embarrassing. From that embarrassment a whole generation of girls and boys found a way to be.[45]

Using sex to sell music, Madonna became the highest-paid pop star in history after signing a $60 million record deal with Time/Warner in 1992. In addition to making her wealthy, Madonna's success opened doors for female musicians in the male-dominated world of rock and roll. A new generation of female artists, including Liz Phair, Gwen Stefani, and Courtney Love, showed Madonna's influences in later years. This pushed MTV to be more receptive to female rockers, which later extended to thoughtful, mellow musicians like Sarah McLachlan and Shawn Colvin.

Prince Generates Controversy

If Madonna was the queen of oversexed, controversial music, Prince was the king. Prince Rogers Nelson was born in Minneapolis, Minnesota, in 1958. He mastered recording techniques by the time he was eighteen and wrote, produced, and played every instrument on a demo record that got him signed by Warner Bros.

In 1979, even before MTV made him a star, Prince generated great controversy with his third album, *Dirty Mind*. He appeared on the cover wearing nothing but underwear and a raincoat, and the album's songs were full of sexually explicit lyrics. Radio programmers refused to play the album, but critics were smitten with Prince's unique "techno funk" sound that combined synthesizers with funk grooves and screaming lead guitar licks.

In 1981 Prince hit the big time with the album *Controversy*. In 1982, Prince's *1999* album produced a number of hits, including "1999," "Delirious," and "Little Red Corvette." Videos of these songs were in heavy MTV rotation in 1984 when Prince's movie *Purple Rain* premiered. *Purple Rain* was a fictionalized account of Prince's teenage years growing up in Minneapolis. The sound track from the movie sold 13 million copies in one year, while the score won Prince an Academy Award.

Prince remained incredibly popular throughout the eighties and nineties, while releasing critically acclaimed albums. Although he generated more controversy when he changed his name to an unpronounceable symbol in 1993, Prince's single-minded dedication to music allowed him to keep his reigning position among rock royalty for years.

Bruce Springsteen's Social Consciousness

With the popularity of Prince and Madonna, it seemed to many rock fans as if sex, controversy, and glamour had taken precedence over substance. Many yearned for a return to rock's roots, which promised listeners that they could find love, heal the world, or achieve their greatest ideals. Music with such promise was seriously lacking during the economic recessions of the 1980s, when many were downsizing their dreams due to hard economic times that shut down factories and small businesses. One of the few voices that offered hope on MTV came from rocker Bruce "The Boss" Springsteen, who spoke of the promise of rock and roll, or "the promise of possibilities; the promise that the search and struggle matter, that they affirm your life. That was the original spirit of rock 'n' roll. And that's what I hope we carry on, a message that no one, nothing has the right to tell you you gotta forfeit your hopes and your dreams."[46]

Springsteen's music synthesized the finest elements of fifties and sixties rock, combining the lonesome, blue feel

Bruce Springsteen performances were a throwback to rock's roots without the glitz and glamour that had become popular with other bands.

of fifties rocker Roy Orbison, the discerning lyrics of Bob Dylan, and a "Wall of Sound" production that layered dozens of instruments atop one another.

The Boss was known for his high-energy stage shows. He appeared wearing simple blue jeans and T-shirts to prove he did not need glitter and glamour to mesmerize an audience. Backed by the hard-rocking E Street Band, Springsteen's marathon shows often lasted three hours and featured the Boss jumping around the stage like an acrobat. When Springsteen's videos of his live concert performances appeared on MTV, it was a breath of fresh air for many rock-and-roll fans.

Springsteen's songs, such as "Hungry Heart" and "Born in the U.S.A.," told the stories of society's outcasts, the down-hearted, the disaffected, and the disenfranchised. Although he was one of the top-selling acts of the 1980s, Springsteen donated much of his time to raising funds for homeless Vietnam veterans, food shelters, the nuclear disarmament movement, Amnesty International, and various environmental causes. In an era of rock-and-roll excess, Springsteen reminded his fans that rock and roll can be about more than ostentatious living and accumulating wealth.

U2's Unforgettable Fire

If Bruce Springsteen was the American social conscious-ness of the 1980s, the band U2 broadened that perspective by giving an international view of the world situation. U2 was born in Ireland in 1978 when singer Bono teamed with guitarist the Edge, bassist Adam Clayton, and drummer Larry Mullen Jr. The group achieved international acclaim with the release of their third album, *War*, in 1983.

War was more openly political than anything released by Springsteen. The song "Sunday Bloody Sunday," driven by a militaristic drumbeat, is about a violent episode that took place in Northern Ireland in January 1972. During a peace-ful protest, the British army opened fire on a crowd of thou-sands, killing thirteen. In 1983 U2 released a video of the band performing "Sunday Bloody Sunday" at the beautiful Red Rocks Amphitheatre in Colorado's Rocky Mountains. While performing the anti-violence anthem, Bono waves a white flag of peace that is seen by the cameras through a heavy crimson mist created by wet weather and hot lights. In 2004 *Rolling Stone* magazine said the "Sunday Bloody Sunday" video performance was one of the fifty moments that changed rock history by making U2 one of the biggest bands in history.

War sold more than a million copies in the United States, giving U2 their first platinum album. The record sold 3 mil-lion copies in England and remains the best-selling concert

album in British history. Stephen Thomas Erlewine, senior music editor for the online AllMusic guide, explains U2's appeal:

> U2 were rock & roll crusaders during an era of synthesized pop. . . . The Edge provided the group with a signature sound by creating sweeping sonic landscapes with his heavily processed, echoed guitars. . . . And their lead singer, Bono, was a frontman with a knack of grand gestures that played better in stadiums than small clubs. It's no accident that footage of Bono parading with a white flag with "Sunday Bloody Sunday" blaring in the background became the defining moment of U2's early career—there rarely was a band that believed so deeply in rock's potential for revolution as U2, and there rarely was a band that didn't care if they appeared foolish in the process.[47]

While U2 was big, they did not become one of the best-selling rock acts in history until they released the album *The Joshua Tree* in 1987. Inspiration for the album came from Bono's 1985 travels to Nicaragua, which was in the midst of a bloody civil war. While in Nicaragua, Bono dodged bullets and bombs and witnessed war crimes. His grim experiences in Central America inspired the lyrics on "Bullet the Blue Sky." Bono sings about airplanes strafing peasant villages, while The Edge imitates bombs whistling with his shrieking guitar. Two other songs on *The Joshua Tree*, "With or Without You" and "I Still Haven't Found What I'm Looking For," gave U2 their first number-one singles in the United States. The group was featured on the cover of *Time* magazine with a headline that labeled them "Rock's Hottest Ticket."

The New Wave of Heavy Metal

U2 was hailed by the press and public for reviving the idealism of the 1960s, while injecting spirituality and compassion into their music. Not everyone embraced these ideals in the late 1980s. Some bands refused to give up their angry punk attitudes, fusing them instead with a new brand of heavy metal.

Like the new romantic movement, the new sound had foundations in Britain, where the hard-core punk attitude was very much alive. Bands that played a no-holds-barred version of heavy metal were labeled the new wave of British heavy metal (NWOBHM), or simply thrash metal. The blues-based music was loud and theatrical, with lyrics drawing inspiration from the dark mythology of witchcraft, demons, black magic, and death. The fast-tempo sound was based on screaming guitar solos and lead singers who delivered vocals in a high-pitch falsetto scream.

Like hard-core punks, thrash metal musicians were generally from the poorer classes and were well acquainted with issues like unemployment, domestic violence, drugs, alcohol, and social alienation. And as with the earlier era of punk rock, there was no wall between the fans and the musician. People at thrash metal concerts pumped their fists in the air, moshed, and jumped headlong from the stage, hoping the crowd would catch them.

With little support from record companies, thrash metal was an underground movement. While MTV and many radio stations initially ignored the music, thrash metal bands toured relentlessly, filling arenas and generating record sales. In this era before the Internet, NWOBHM fans stayed informed through cheap paper magazines called fanzines, which carried information about upcoming concerts, their favorite bands, thrash fashion, and other news.

Thrash metal took off in London, England, during the early 1980s with bands such as Judas Priest, Iron Maiden, and Motorhead. Around the same time, Australian metal rockers AC/DC hit the British top ten with the album *Highway to Hell.* AC/DC continued its success in the United States, hitting the U.S. top ten with its next albums, *Back in Black* and *For Those About to Rock (We Salute You).* Music journalist Chris Smith explains the appeal of AC/DC to American rock fans in the early 1980s:

> AC/DC struck out for American shores to remind everybody what heavy metal was all about: alienated teenagers bobbing their heads in unison to crunchy power chords, banshee screams, and a thundering rhythm section. No vain posturing as in the rapidly fading phenomenon of disco, no angry politics like the self-imploding punk genre, no ironic social awareness like the trendsetting new wavers, and no heavily polished arena filler like the overproduced corporate groups that were hijacking America's radios. Just loud rock played with wild abandon.[48]

Thrash Metal Speeds Up

Bands like AC/DC and Iron Maiden spread their influence to American bands, and by the mid-1980s the Los Angeles–based group Metallica had added a new twist to thrash metal. They played their music as fast as possible in a style dubbed speed metal. Metallica released the album *Kill 'em All* in 1983, and by 1988 the band hit the top ten album charts, selling 9 million copies of *And Justice for All.*

Metallica's success opened doors for dozens of other thrash metal bands, and by the late 1980s music media outlets could no longer ignore the moneymaking power of the heaviest metal. Radio stations began playing the songs,

Guns N' Roses' Raw Rock

Heavy metal became a mainstream musical phenomenon in the late 1980s thanks to one of the era's most popular bands, Guns N' Roses (GNR). The group is described by Stephen Thomas Erlewine, senior music editor for the AllMusic website:

At a time when pop was dominated by dance music and pop-metal, Guns N' Roses brought raw, ugly rock & roll crashing back into the charts. They were not nice boys; nice boys don't play rock & roll. They were ugly, misogynistic, and violent; they were also funny, vulnerable, and occasionally sensitive, as their breakthrough hit, "Sweet Child O' Mine," showed. While Slash and Izzy Stradlin ferociously spit out dueling guitar riffs worthy of Aerosmith or the Stones, Axl Rose screeched out his tales of sex, drugs, and apathy in the big city. Meanwhile, bassist Duff McKagan and drummer Steven Adler were a limber rhythm section who kept the music loose and powerful.

Stephen Thomas Erlewine, "Guns N' Roses." AllMusic, 2011, www.allmusic.com/artist/guns-n-roses-p4416/biography.

while MTV ran videos by thrash metal rockers Anthrax, Def Leppard, Megadeth, Poison, Ratt, and Slaughter. The sound quickly became part of mainstream rock and roll. One of most successful mainstream metal bands was Guns N' Roses (GNR). Its 1987 video for the song "Sweet Child O' Mine" received heavy rotation on MTV and helped push sales of the GNR album *Appetite for Destruction* into the stratosphere.

Red Hot Chili Rock

Metal and punk came together with funk, blues, and psychedelic rock in Los Angeles, California, when vocalist

The Red Hot Chili Peppers' eclectic blending of a wide range of musical styles helped propel them to stardom.

Anthony Kiedis and bassist "Flea" Balzary formed the Red Hot Chili Peppers in 1983 with an ever-changing cast of guitarists and drummers. The band's sound, sometimes referred to as funk metal or funk-n-roll, was formed around a genre called dirty funk, pioneered in the 1970s by George Clinton's various groups that were known collectively as Parliament-Funkadelic or P-Funk. Dirty funk blended the psychedelic fuzz-guitar style of Jimi Hendrix with the funky rhythms of soul singer James Brown. The Red Hot Chili Peppers added the driving guitars and up-tempo drums of thrash metal, along with other elements described by *Spin* magazine in 1984:

> The Chili Peppers' music is an unprecedented blend of styles mixing [the 1950s country music of] Hank Williams with rap, Led Zeppelinoid arpeggios [harmonies] with R & B chicken-scratch guitar; produc-

ing a sort of seamless fusion of hardcore, Delta Blues, hip hop and straight-ahead rock. They are very black, very white, and never gray. Onstage, bare chests, arms and legs smeared with dayglo paint, wearing weird hats and masks, moving like pinballs or witch docs or barefoot on hot asphalt, they're wild as Iggy and the Stooges or P-Funk.[49]

When *Spin* published this enthusiastic review, the Chili Peppers were barely known outside of Los Angeles, where the band's wild shows made them popular fixtures on the club circuit. The band finally achieved major stardom in 1991 with the release of the album *Blood Sugar Sex Magik*, which featured the surprisingly tender ballad "Under the Bridge." Videos of this song and the funk-rap-metal monster "Give It Away" were in constant rotation on MTV. This brought the Chili Peppers to a large, mainstream audience, and ultimately influenced a generation of funk-punk-metal artists like Linkin Park, Korn, and Limp Bizkit, who are referred to as nu metal.

Assailed by Social Critics

The Red Hot Chili Peppers often wrote explicit lyrics, and every member of the band was treated for heroin addiction at some point. Heavy metal bands were also known to sing about drugs and sex, along with Satan and witchcraft. This trend led conservative social critics to assail many of the most popular bands of the era, claiming that their songs' words drove teens to irresponsible sex, drug use, and even suicide. Despite these concerns, millions of records were snapped up by teens who delighted in shocking adults with the harsh new sounds. As a result, funk punk and heavy metal bands remained a constant irritant to parents and authority figures throughout the eighties, nineties, and beyond.

Alternative Rock

By the mid-1990s rock music genres had split and recombined into numerous new styles. Musical acts were labeled punk metal, West Coast punk, funk-n-roll, funk metal, country punk, and countless other fusions. As Larry Starr and Christopher Waterman write, "From jangle-pop to trip hop, psychobilly to thrashcore, the decade saw a splintering of genres that exceeded anything previously experienced in the history of American popular music."[50]

Some of these styles were pioneered by a few bands in a single locale like a college town. The music was promoted by small independent record labels. The fused musical styles were considered grassroots, created and supported by small groups of people with common interests and backgrounds. Members of these isolated musical communities proudly identified themselves as part of an underground, independent, or alternative movement. As a result, individuals buying records as diverse as country punk, thrash core, and funk metal came to be identified by a few all-encompassing terms: indie, alternative, or alt-rock.

Originally, alt-rockers rejected the pop music promoted by the entertainment industry and enjoyed by mainstream America. Alternative music, as Starr and Waterman explain, was "thought by its supporters to be local as opposed to corporate, homemade as opposed to mass-produced, and genuine as opposed to artificial."[51]

R.E.M. Feels Fine

Whatever the attitudes of the alt-rock underground, the music industry was well aware of independent music. Record companies had their own singular definition of alternative rock: the sound popularized by the group R.E.M. in the late 1980s. R.E.M. embodied important elements that would come to be identified with alternative rock. They were local musical heroes in a small college town, signed by what was then an indie record label. R.E.M.'s music combined punk, folk, and light-metal power chords into catchy tunes.

R.E.M. popularized alternative rock in the late 1980s. Michael Stipe (left) and guitarist Peter Buck (right) are seen here performing in Germany in 2008.

R.E.M. was formed in 1980 by singer Michael Stipe, guitarist Peter Buck, bassist Mike Mills, and drummer Bill Berry. The group combined several styles that would seem completely incompatible. R.E.M.'s sound mixed the jingle-jangle sound of folk-rock acoustic guitars popularized by the band the Byrds in the mid-sixties, the proto-punk of the Velvet Underground from the late sixties, and the hard-driving punk rock beat of the mid-seventies.

The members of R.E.M. were students at the University of Georgia in Athens, and they quickly became a favorite local band. The group was signed by independent record label I.R.S., and their 1983 debut album, *Murmur*, was picked as the record of the year by *Rolling Stone*. Four years later, R.E.M. released *Document*, which features "It's the End of the World As We Know It (And I Feel Fine)." In the song, Stipe recites rapid-fire, fear-inducing, stream-of-consciousness lyrics that mention hurricanes, book burnings, bloodletting, and earthquakes. The infectious sing-along chorus helped make the song R.E.M.'s first hit single and pushed *Document* to the top of the album charts. The song "The One I Love" was the second number-one single from the album, and videos from the album made R.E.M. stars on MTV.

Try and Fool Them

While few might have been aware of alt-rock in the early 1990s, record companies could not help but notice. R.E.M, along with other unique bands such as the Red Hot Chili Peppers, Nine Inch Nails, and Sonic Youth, were selling records. While their sounds varied from head-nodding rock to anguished screams and electronic noise, this was music that could be very profitable to record companies. To exploit the new styles and the consumer trend towards independently produced music, record companies created dozens of fake independent record labels. As one unnamed executive for a major entertainment conglomerate stated, his company created an entire alternative division because, "[There are] kids that will only buy records that are on an indie label. . . . [Which] is why we sometimes concoct labels to try and fool them."[52]

The major record companies also bought up small independent labels. People who worked for these companies were viewed as local talent scouts who knew the regional music scenes and were positioned to discover the next R.E.M. While indie rockers and music fans criticized the situation, Larry Starr and Christopher Waterman write, "It became difficult to sustain a purely economic definition of alternative music as music that doesn't make money. To put it another way, the fact that a band's music, song lyrics, appearance, and ideological stance are anticommerical doesn't mean that they can't sell millions of records and thereby help to generate huge corporate profits."[53]

Seattle Grunge

In the rainy city of Seattle, Washington, singer-songwriter-guitarist Kurt Cobain and bassist Krist Novoselic watched the actions of major record companies with distain. The two men formed the group Nirvana in 1987, the same year R.E.M. became rock superstars. After adding drummer Dave Grohl in 1990, Nirvana's sound gelled into a blend of thick, sludgy, distorted guitar textures mixed with hard-hitting punk rock rhythms. The songs, written by Cobain, merged hard-core attitude with the 1960s garage band sound exemplified by the Troggs in "Wild Thing" or the Standelles in "Dirty Water."

Nirvana's sound was also heard from Seattle bands like Soundgarden, Mudhoney, and Pearl Jam. The style came to be known as the Seattle sound, or grunge. Most people in the Seattle alternative music scene hated the term *grunge*, which was associated with gooey filth. Jack Endino, who produced Nirvana and Soundgarden, rejects the term *grunge* and says the Seattle sound was "a resurgence of classic rock—the classic rock song structures, chord sequences, melodies. All the ingredients of classic '70s rock, with maybe a little bit of '80s punk attitude thrown into the recipe. Nobody dressed funny, and nobody had funny haircuts. . . . [Nobody] had *any* haircuts."[54]

A true independent record label called Sub Pop, founded in 1989, was at the center of the Seattle music scene. Sub

A Cloud of Options

Until the mid-1990s, when the World Wide Web became a major force in disseminating music, alternative rock lovers could only access their favorite sounds through small college radio stations or CD purchases. Information about obscure indie bands was largely restricted to fanzines. Nitsuh Abebe, columnist for the popular alternative rock website Pitchfork, explains how the growth of the Internet in the first decade of the twenty-first century made alt-rock music widely available to a large audience:

> I'll spare you a long old-mannish digression about the things I had to do, pre-Internet, to engage with the music I wanted to hear; it was a constant and hilariously archaic scramble. But these days, these things float past you everywhere, and I'm hard-pressed to think of many acts I'd recommend that you couldn't very casually, within two minutes of web-searching, check out right on your computer. More and more, we define ourselves—or pride ourselves, or at least "express" ourselves—via our skills in picking interesting things out of that cloud of [Internet] options. We probably shouldn't be surprised that somewhere in this process, "indie" completed its trip from being the province of freaks and geeks to something with cachet—something that appeals to people's sense of themselves as *discerning*.

Quoted in Ann Powers and Daphne Carr, eds. *Best Music Writing 2010*. New York: Da Capo Press, 2011, p. 128.

Pop was an abbreviation of *Subterranean Pop*, a fanzine created by label founder Bruce Pavitt in Olympia, Washington, in the early 1980s. In 1986 Pavitt joined with Jonathan Poneman to launch Sub Pop Records in order to distribute cassettes and short vinyl albums, known as EPs (extended plays), made by local musicians.

Smells Like Nirvana

Sub Pop signed Nirvana in 1989. The group recorded its first album *Bleach* in one week, at a cost of only $600. This was an incredibly quick and inexpensive production during an era when major bands were spending half a million dollars over the course of twelve months to make a record. Nirvana's fast, cheap sessions paid off incredibly well. *Bleach* sold more than thirty-five thousand copies. As part of the album's promotion, Sub Pop published a jokey, ironic press release:

> NIRVANA sees the underground scene as becoming stagnant and more accessible to big league capitalist pig major labels. But does NIRVANA feel a moral duty to fight this cancerous evil? NO WAY! We want to cash in and suck up to the big wigs in hopes that . . . SOON we will need groupie repellant."[55]

Despite the sarcastic tone of the press release, Nirvana signed with a major label, DGC Records, in 1990. With the release of the album *Nevermind* in 1991, Nirvana took alternative rock to mainstream America. Cobain, who had become addicted to heroin, projected a vulnerable yet volatile image for the album. *Nevermind* features his intense, emotional lyrics backed by raucous, intense, angst-ridden music. Driven by the catchy single "Smells Like Teen Spirit," which became the first anthem of grunge, *Nevermind* eventually sold more than 7 million copies in the United States alone. The memorable video for "Smells Like Teen Spirit" was in heavy rotation on MTV and helped Nirvana become the first grunge band to be featured on the cover of *Rolling Stone*.

Kurt Cobain of Nirvana was the face of the Seattle grunge movement in the late 1980s and early 1990s.

Rock-and-Roll Suicide

The success of Nirvana and grunge helped push Pearl Jam to the top of the charts. The group's 1992 album *Ten* sold 9

The popularity of bands such as Pearl Jam helped drive the grunge sound to mainstream audiences.

million copies, propelled by the rich, soaring vocals of lead singer Eddie Vedder. In 1993 Pearl Jam broke first-week sales records as their second album, *Vs.*, sold almost a million copies within a week of its release.

With Pearl Jam and Nirvana topping the charts, the grunge fashion style spread across America. Grunge rockers wore heavy Doc Martens boots, ripped flannel shirts, torn jeans, knit caps, and unkempt hair. Although the so-called style was simply a practical way for poor musicians who lived in Seattle's cold, rainy climate to keep warm, grunge outfits were featured in a *Vogue* magazine fashion spread. Several big-name New York fashion designers adopted the look for their fashion shows.

Kurt Cobain felt personally responsible for the commercialization of grunge, a style of music based on the rejection of greed, hypocrisy, trendiness, and lies. Cobain became deeply depressed, stressed by his sudden stardom, his rocky relationship with his wife, Courtney Love, and his struggles with heroin addiction. After surviving an overdose of champagne and tranquilizers in March 1994, Cobain killed himself with a shotgun blast to the head on April 5, 1994.

He died alone in his Seattle mansion. Like Jimi Hendrix, Janis Joplin, and Jim Morrison, Cobain was twenty-seven years old at the time of his death.

Scrunge

After Kurt Cobain's suicide, countless bands were attracted to the grunge style because it was seen as a way to stardom. This launched the post-grunge, or scrunge, era with bands like Bush, from England, and Candlebox, from Seattle. These groups took elements of the grunge sound but cleaned up the sludgy guitars, wrote less angst-ridden lyrics, and left alternative's indie values behind. The result was radio-friendly grunge with wide appeal.

Grunge and scrunge were absorbed into the broad alternative rock category, which became extremely popular after Nirvana's album *Nevermind* was released in 1991. As a monthly columnist for the comprehensive online alternative music website Pitchfork, Nitsuh Abebe was an eyewitness to the alt-rock explosion in the early part of the first decade of the twenty-first century:

> Alt-rock more or less party-crashed the mainstream, and mainstream audiences party-crashed it right back, and that sent everyone under the indie umbrella elbowing and shoving for new space. The kinds of alt-rock that got popular tended to be very straightforward: fuzzy, glossy rock songs; brash, masculine grunge; blocky, bright, and ironic pop. . . . And after a while of that, as everyone settled from the shake-up of the alt-rock boom, this whole "indie" audience really did regroup around liking certain types of things.[56]

"Groovy Trippy" Beck

No one exemplified the new sound of alt-rock better than Beck Hanson, who was born in Los Angles in 1970. Known simply as Beck, he created a hybrid style of alternative musical collages influenced by a wide range of styles that included rap, blues, rock, country, and even movie sound tracks.

The Women of Lilith Fair

Canadian singer Sarah McLachlan wrote thoughtful, well-crafted songs that helped her 1993 platinum-selling album *Fumbling Towards Ecstasy* spend sixty-two weeks on the pop charts. Despite her success, McLachlan was fed up with the music business, especially the concert industry. During this era, bookers refused to put more than one female artist on a tour, and women were only used as warmup acts for male-dominated bands. McLachlan set out to change music industry sexism in 1997, producing Lilith Fair, a rock festival in which all of the featured acts were women. The first Lilith Fair featured a who's who of award-winning women rockers of the era, including Jewel, Shawn Colvin, Heather Nova, the Indigo Girls, Fiona Apple, Sheryl Crow, Suzanne Vega, Tracy Chapman, Bonnie Raitt, and Emmylou Harris. The concert tour surprised everyone by grossing $16 million in thirty-eight shows. This was nearly double the take of the male-dominated alternative music festival Lollapalooza. Lilith Fair continued in 1998 and 1999.

The success of Lilith Fair, which attracted a predominately female audience, brought women back into the mainstream of music and gave voice to great talents that until that time had been too often ignored by the music industry. McLachlan tried to revive Lilith Fair in 2010, but about half of the shows were canceled due to poor ticket sales.

Inspired by the success of the Beastie Boys, a white-boy hip-hop group of the late 1980s, Beck tried to record a rap song. After laying down some rhymes in the studio, however, the results were terrible. This inspired Beck to improvise the verse "I'm a loser baby, so why don't you kill me."[57] This line formed the basis for Beck's alt-rap single "Loser" from the album *Mellow Gold*. "Loser" peaked at number ten on the *Billboard* Hot 100 charts and the "I'm a loser" chorus became a mid-1990s catchphrase. Critics gave Beck high praise. According to Chris Norris, senior staff writer for *Spin*, Beck was "knighted [as] . . . a generation's consolation prize after the death of Kurt Cobain."[58] Beck fans might disagree with this assessment since his music almost always exhibits irony, sarcasm, and humor—qualities lacking in Cobain's angst-ridden sound.

Beck had strong artistic ties to his grandfather, Al Hanson, a famed collage artist. Hanson was part of the Fluxus movement of the 1950s and early 1960s. Fluxus artists were amateur do-it-yourself types who could be compared to alternative rockers. They bucked the popular artistic trends and took bits and pieces of various media, such as ads, playing cards, words, photos, and so on, and combined them into unique works. After Beck dropped out of high school in the mid-1980s, he spent time with his grandfather in Germany.

Whatever the degree of Al Hanson's influence on Beck's work, the 1996 album *Odelay* is something of a Fluxus masterpiece. While creating the album, Beck pasted together music and a dizzying array of short segments of sounds from earlier recordings, or samples. Chris Norris describes the album: "*Odelay* defined much of the sound and attitude of the post-grunge, pre-bling 90s; groovy trippy, sprawling, neo-retro, retro-neo, and fully loaded with jingles, hooks, breakbeats, Moogs [synthesizers], Troggs, Schubert, and titles like 'Devil's Haircut.'"[59]

For his next album, 1998's *Mutations*, Beck recorded a song a day for eleven days. This low-key, acoustic-sounding album was also a musical collage that combined country, blues, and Brazilian bossa nova and tropicalia styles with 1960s-era Moog synthesizers, strings, and Latin percussion. While *Odelay* was hip-hop oriented, Beck showed off his musical skills on his later album *Mutations*, utilizing unusual and complex chord patterns and Dylan-esque lyrics on songs like "Cold Brains" and "Dead Melodies."

In 1999 Beck won a Grammy for Best Alternative Music Performance for *Mutations*. Later in the year, he released *Midnight Vultures*, his most ambitious album to date. Inspired by 1970s funk, David Bowie, and Prince, the album combines soaring, diving synthesizer lines, horns, screaming wah-wah guitars, and throbbing drums. While

Beck tries to imitate the sexy vocal style of Prince, his humorous irony is on full display in songs like "Nicotine and Gravy," "Sexx Laws," and "Debra." Beck called *Midnight Vultures* "a party record with dumb sounds and dumb songs and dumb lyrics."[60] Whether he was being modest or ironic, few alt-rockers have exhibited the talent and lyrical genius the Grammy-winning, platinum-selling artist highlighted on his series of unique alt-rock albums.

American Idiots

Beck's inward-looking lyrics and complex sound textures stand in sharp contrast to Green Day, another alternative music Grammy winner of the era. Green Day is made up of guitarist-vocalist Billie Joe Armstrong, bassist Mike Dirnt, and drummer Tré Cool, all born in 1972. The band gained a large following in the early-1990s punk scene in Berkeley, California, playing music that was political and critical of American society. The group became a sensation with the multiplatinum 1993 album *Dookie*, which was credited for single-handedly resurrecting punk rock for a new generation.

Green Day's stripped-down, Ramones-style sound of hard-strummed power chords, percolating bass, and explosive drumming drives Armstrong's clever lyrics, sung in what sounds like a fake British accent. The group's guitar hooks and melodies are surprisingly catchy, which led critics to call Green Day pop punk, or more derisively, mall punk or snot core.

Whatever the labels applied to the band, their peppy songs on *Dookie* and their subsequent album, *Nimrod*, explore the neuroses of a generation raised in broken homes with broken dreams. Green Day reached its mainstream peak with the song "Good Riddance (Time of Your Life)," which was played on the last episode of the immensely popular TV sitcom *Seinfeld* that was seen by 76 million viewers in 1998. The stark song, with Armstrong singing and strumming an acoustic guitar solo, has a sentimental quality expressed by the singer looking back nostalgically at a happier period of his life. Because of its bittersweet, emotional content, the

Billie Joe Armstrong of Green Day performs on Broadway in their semi-autobiographical musical American Idiot.

song was played at nearly every high school and university graduation in following years.

After the tragic terrorist attacks on the World Trade Center and the Pentagon on September 11, 2001, Armstrong believed the political climate in America had become repressive and paranoid. His reaction was to write the album *American Idiot*, which was released in 2004.

American Idiot is a rock opera—an album in which all the interrelated songs tell a story. *American Idiot* is about an antihero named Jesus of Suburbia, who lives on soda pop and Ritalin. He inhabits a world consumed by fear, hypocrisy, pain, and evil politicians, described in songs like "City of the Damned," "Tales From Another Broken Home," and an ode to the president titled "American Idiot." The album sold 14 million copies. When the band toured to support the album, they sold out nearly every one of the 150 dates from the United States to South America, Europe, and Australia. The tour was documented on the best-selling DVD *Bullet in a Bible*, and one of the shows, recorded in front of one hundred thirty thousand people in London in 2005, was released as a music CD.

Breakdown

Green Day released the follow-up to *American Idiot* in 2009. Titled *21st Century Breakdown*, it explored similar themes. Commenting on the record, guitarist-vocalist Billie Joe Armstrong stated, "Our country—and the world for that matter—is in the worst shape I've ever seen it. But there's this sense of hope that people have. And there's a *lot* of confusion. It's the strangest time. And that's kind of what *21st Century Breakdown* is about."[61] Green Day scored another hit with *21st Century Breakdown*. The album went triple platinum and was awarded the 2010 Grammy Award for Best Rock Album.

In 2009 the rock opera *American Idiot* was turned into a stage musical, which had a successful run at the Berkeley Repertory Theater in Berkeley, California. The play moved to Broadway in New York City the following year, closing in April 2011 after 422 performances. Green Day members were not in the play, but Armstrong appeared onstage a few times in the role of St. Jimmy. *American Idiot* received a Tony nomination for Best Musical and won a Grammy Award for Best Musical Show Album.

Vampires and Critics

By the early years of the second decade of the twenty-first century, alternative rock had come to encompass so many sounds and styles it was almost impossible to define. There were clever, quirky, guitar-based bands like the Foo Fighters, Blink-182, and Kings of Leon, alt-country acts like Wilco,

"Slashed Strings, Blaring Brass, Pounded Percussion"

In 2011 Arcade Fire's album *The Suburbs* won the prestigious Grammy Award for Album of the Year. The seven-member alt-rock band is made up of the husband-wife team of Win Butler (guitar, vocals) and Régine Chassagne (multi-instrumentalist, vocals), along with Jeremy Gara (drums), Richard Parry (bass), Sarah Neufeld (violin), Will Butler (keyboard), and Tim Kingsbury (guitar). Featuring orchestral songs that might include accordion, French horn, harp, mandolin, cello, violin, and even the xylophone, Arcade Fire is quirky and unique even in the eccentric world of alternative rock music. *Rolling Stone* contributor Jim Macnie describes Arcade Fire's music as "cathedrals of sound . . . a mix of slashed strings, blaring brass,

pounded percussion, and Win Butler's spooked croon."

The buzz around Arcade Fire began soon after the group released its first album, *Funeral*, in 2004. The band's fan base continued to expand with the release of 2007's *Neon Bible*, recorded in an abandoned church that the group turned into a recording studio. *Neon Bible* debuted at number two on the Billboard 200, and has been credited in the music press for attracting renewed public interest in alternative rock. In addition to winning a Grammy in 2011, *The Suburbs* received twenty-two other major awards from the BBC, MTV, *Time*, *NME*, *Rolling Stone*, Pitchfork, and other media outlets.

Jim Macnie, "Arcade Fire." *Rolling Stone*, 2011, www.rollingstone.com/music/artists/arcade-fire/biographym.

alternative hip-hop from Gnarls Barkley, and the seven-piece symphonic sound of Arcade Fire.

The group Vampire Weekend proved to be one of the most talked-about bands, but for an unusual reason. Unlike the post-punk rock groups flooding college radio stations in the latter part of the first decade of the twenty-first century, Vampire Weekend, known as VW to their fans, sounded happy, light, and breezy. Their first two albums, *Vampire Weekend* and *Contra*, mix the fizzy beats of African pop, reggae, and calypso music with harpsichords, strings, and clean pop-rock guitar. Its band members were all students at Columbia University in New York, and the group generated criticism for writing lyrics that would appeal to privileged

Vampire Weekend's light and breezy style proved popular in the early 2000s, although alt-rock was losing ground to teen pop and hip hop.

preppies. As Nitsuh Abebe writes, "I was pretty charmed with Vampire Weekend's debut, but I was also charmed by the way some people who hated it didn't just dislike the music: some of them objected, viscerally, to the very idea that indie bands would even be like that."[62]

The visceral reaction to an accessible album filled with catchy tunes showed alternative rock values remained important to some even in the early part of the second decade of the twenty-first century. Even as critics tussled over the authenticity of Vampire Weekend, the alt-rock style was losing its commercial appeal. Beginning in the early part of the first decade of the twenty-first century, alt music sales figures began to lag behind those of teen pop and hip-hop.

Arcade Fire is an example of alt-rock's fading appeal. Although its album *The Suburbs* won a Grammy for Album of the Year in 2011, the record only peaked at number twelve on the *Billboard* Top 200 album charts. By comparison, Britney Spears's 2011 album *Femme Fatale* debuted at number one and stayed in the top ten for more than a month.

Of course, in an era where illegal file sharing is rampant, it is hard to determine how many people enjoy listening to *The Suburbs*. During the first decade of the twenty-first century, more than half of all music consumers admitted to illegally downloading songs from the Internet. Even those who purchased music bought fewer CDs in favor of single songs from online music stores like iTunes. CDs provide a much greater profit to record companies and, coupled with illegal downloading, the years during the middle of the decade were the worst ever in the music business.

Troubles for Alt-Rock

During the first decade of the twenty-first century, several changes caused a downward trend in alt-rock music sales. While legal digital song downloads from online stores like iTunes increased 150 percent between 2004 and 2005—to 325 million—consumers bought 48 million fewer albums than the previous year. CDs are much more profitable than single song downloads, meaning bands and record companies made far less money. This prompted Simon Renshaw, manager of the country group the Dixie Chicks, to comment: "With digital technology, everyone's figured out that a business built only on the manufacture, distribution, and sale of CDs has ended. The traditional model can't continue."

Alternative rock faced more problems in 2008 when alt-rock FM radio stations in the nation's biggest cities went off the air. In Los Angeles, the alt-rock giant Indie 102 switched to Internet-only broadcasting, while stations with similar formats in New York City and Boston, Massachusetts, switched to Top 40 and sports talk. With this trend, and the growth of digital music downloads, many alt-rockers faced difficult financial times.

Quoted in Brian and Evan Serpick, "Music Biz Laments 'Worst Year Ever.'" *Rolling Stone*, January 13, 2006, www.rollingstone.com/music/news/music-biz-laments-worst-year-ever-20060113.

And the Bands Play On

Alt-rock bands might not sell as many CDs as groups did in previous eras, but the music has become a cultural staple and a major part of the entertainment industry. Popular bands supported themselves with concert tours and sales of songs for TV commercials and movies. The Vampire Weekend single "Holiday" is heard in Tommy Hilfiger and Honda commercials. Another of their songs, "Jonathan Low," appeared on the sound track to *The Twilight Saga: Eclipse*.

Rock music in the first decade of the twenty-first century has morphed into almost anything its fans want it to be. Instead of hearing a few artists such as Elvis Presley or the Beatles dominating the airwaves as they had in a previous era, modern rock fans found music of obscure bands on the Internet and followed their careers online. This meant musicians no longer needed record companies in order to be heard. Bands were producing songs cheaply and efficiently on their home computers, promoting them on their home pages, and selling them from digital music stores. This allowed music of nearly every style or combination of styles available to the greatest number of people. With tens of thousands of songs available at the click of a mouse, the words sung by legendary rocker Neil Young in 1979 are as true now as they were in the 1950s: "Rock and roll will never die."

NOTES

Chapter 1: Good Rockin' Tonight

1. W.C. Handy. *Father of the Blues.* New York: Macmillan, 1941, p. 74.
2. James Miller. *Flowers in the Dustbin: The Rise of Rock and Roll, 1947–1977.* New York: Simon & Schuster, 1999, p. 92.
3. Quoted in Robert K. Oermann. *A Century of Country.* New York: TV Books, 1999, p. 136.
4. Quoted in Gene N. Landrum. *Paranoia & Power: Fear & Fame of Entertainment Icons.* New York: Morgan James Publishing, 2007, p. 59.
5. Quoted in William McKeen (ed). *Rock and Roll is Here to Stay.* New York: W.W. Norton & Company, 2000, p. 29.
6. Quoted in Oermann. *A Century of Country*, p. 142.
7. Quoted in Linda Martin and Kerry Segrave. *Anti-Rock.* Hamden, CT: Archon Books, 1988, p. 76.
8. Buddy Holly. "Buddy Holly Quotes," Bookrags, 2011, www.book rags.com/quotes/ Buddy_Holly.
9. Quoted in David P. Szatmary. *Rockin' in Time: A Social History of Rock and Roll.* New York: Schirmer Books, 1996, p. 18.
10. Quoted in Martin and Segrave. *Anti-Rock*, p. 73.
11. Quoted in Mark Jacobson. "Chuck Berry, the Father of Rock, Turns 75," *Rolling Stone*, December 6, 2001, p. 80.
12. Quoted in Martin and Segrave. *Anti-Rock*, p. 44.

Chapter 2: Sixties Rock and Roll, Folk, and Soul

13. Quoted in The Beatles. *The Beatles Anthology.* San Francisco: Chronicle Books, 2000, p. 49.
14. Quoted in Pete Shotten and Nicholas Schaffner. *John Lennon In My Life.* New York: Stein and Day, 1983, p. 69.
15. Shotten and Schaffner. *John Lennon*, p. 68.
16. Michael Gray. *Song & Dance Man III: The Art of Bob Dylan.* London: Cassell, 2000, p. 4.
17. Gray. *Song & Dance Man III*, p. 4.
18. Quoted in Anthony DeCurtis, James Henke, and Holly George-Warren, eds. *The Rolling Stone Illustrated History of Rock & Roll.*

New York: Random House, 1992, p. 281.

Chapter 3: Rock Gets Experienced

19. Quoted in Jann Wenner, ed. *20 Years of Rolling Stone: What A Long, Strange Trip It's Been.* New York: Straight Arrow Publishers, 1987, p. 37.
20. George Martin. *With a Little Help from My Friends: The Making of Sgt. Pepper.* New York: Little, Brown and Company, 1994, p. 157.
21. Quoted in David Brackett, ed. *The Pop, Rock, and Soul Reader.* New York: Oxford University Press, 2005, p. 222.
22. Quoted in Szatmary. *Rockin' in Time*, p. 153.
23. Quoted in Jim DeRogatis. *Kaleidoscope Eyes.* New York: Citadel Press, 1996, p. 54.
24. Quoted in DeRogatis. *Kaleidoscope Eyes*, p. 57.
25. Ed Ward, Geoffrey Stokes, and Ken Tucker. *Rock of Ages: The Rolling Stone History of Rock.* New York: Rolling Stone Press, 1986, p. 486.
26. Quoted in DeRogatis. *Kaleidoscope Eyes*, p. 72.
27. Quoted in Miller. *Flowers in the Dustbin*, p. 299.

Chapter 4: The Psychotic World of Punk

28. Quoted in Holly George-Warren, ed. *Rolling Stone: The Decades of Rock & Roll.* San Francisco: Chronicle Books, 2001, p. 117.
29. Quoted in George-Warren. *Rolling Stone*, p. 119.
30. Larry Starr and Christopher Waterman. *American Popular Music from Minstrelsy to MTV.* New York: Oxford University Press, 2003, p. 332.
31. Quoted in Szatmary. *Rockin' in Time*, p. 226.
32. Quoted in Starr and Waterman. *American Popular Music*, p. 368.
33. Quoted in Tricia Henry. *Break All the Rules: Punk Rock and the Making of a Style.* Ann Arbor, MI: UMI Research Press, 1989, p. 57.
34. Quoted in Henry. *Break All the Rules*, p. 59.
35. Quoted in Clinton Heylin. *Babylon's Burning: From Punk to Grunge.* New York: Conongate, 2007, p. 83.
36. Quoted in Heylin. *Babylon's Burning*, p. 90.
37. Starr and Waterman. *American Popular Music*, p. 375.
38. Quoted in Szatmary. *Rockin' in Time*, p. 274.
39. Quoted in Szatmary. *Rockin' in Time*, pp. 274–275.
40. Quoted in Szatmary. *Rockin' in Time*, p. 277.

Chapter 5: From Pop Rock to the Heaviest Metal

41. Quoted in Brackett. *The Pop, Rock, and Soul Reader*, p. 386.
42. Quoted in Brackett. *The Pop, Rock, and Soul Reader*, p. 392.

43. Greg Tate. "I'm White! What's Wrong With Michael Jackson," Village Voice, July 26, 2009, http://blogs.villagevoice.com/music/2009/06/from_the_voice_2.php.

44. Quoted in Martin and Segrave. *Anti-Rock*, p. 283.

45. Quoted in Chris Smith. *101 Albums That Changed Popular Music*. New York: Oxford University Press, 2009, pp. 178–179.

46. Quoted in Smith. *101 Albums*, p. 172.

47. Stephen Thomas Erlewine. "U2," iTunes, 2011, http://itunes.apple.com/us/artist/u2/id78500.

48. Smith. *101 Albums*, p. 156.

49. Quoted in Smith. *101 Albums*, p. 217.

Chapter 6: Alternative Rock

50. Starr and Waterman. *American Popular Music*, p. 446.

51. Starr and Waterman. *American Popular Music*, p. 446.

52. Quoted in Keith Negus. *Producing Pop: Culture and Conflict in the Popular Music Industry*. London: Hodder Arnold, 1992, p. 16.

53. Starr and Waterman. *American Popular Music*, p. 447.

54. Greg Prato. *Grunge is Dead*. Toronto: ECW Press, 2009, pp. 242–243.

55. Quoted in Starr and Waterman. *American Popular Music*, p. 453.

56. Quoted in Ann Powers and Daphne Carr, eds. *Best Music Writing 2010*. New York: Da Capo Press, 2011, pp. 124–125.

57. Quoted in Will Hermes and Sia Michel, eds. *Spin: 20 Years of Alternative Music*. New York: Three Rivers Press, 2005, p. 179.

58. Quoted in Hermes and Michel. *Spin*, p. 179.

59. Quoted in Hermes and Michel. *Spin*, p. 179.

60. Quoted in John Pareles. "Midnight Vultures by Beck," *Rolling Stone*, November 27, 2002, www.rollingstone.com/music/albumreviews/midnite-vultures-20021127.

61. Quoted in Clark Collis. "Green Day's Billie Joe Armstrong," Music Mix, April 2, 2009, http://music-mix.ew.com/2009/04/02/billie-joe-arms.

62. Quoted in Powers and Carr. *Best Music Writing 2010*, p. 129.

AC/DC

Highway to Hell, 1979

The last album lead singer Bon Scott recorded with AC/DC before his death, *Highway to Hell* features the classic heavy metal sound that made the group favorites of headbangers across the globe.

For Those About to Rock (We Salute You), 1981

Arcade Fire

Neon Bible, 2007

Recorded in a church the band was renovating, Arcade Fire's breakout album is a symphonic masterpiece of clamor rock, with rich, warped, desperate textures filled out with cello, harp, viola, brass, and choir arrangements.

The Beatles

A Hard Day's Night, 1964

Rubber Soul, 1965

Sgt. Pepper's Lonely Hearts Club Band, 1967

Sgt. Pepper is one of the most important albums in history, and one that forever changed pop music.

Magical Mystery Tour, 1967

While critics hated the film *Magical Mystery Tour*, the accompanying album contains classic gems from the Beatles' psychedelic era, including "I Am the Walrus," "All You Need is Love," "Baby You're a Rich Man," and "Strawberry Fields Forever."

Beck

Odelay, 1996

Beck's fifth studio album, and the one that brought him international acclaim with the hit single "Where It's At," this alt-rock masterpiece boasts timeless classics like "Devil's Haircut" and "New Pollution." It has been called anti-folk and country rap, but it is all Beck, with jangling guitars, crazy sound samples, and hilarious, ironic lyrics.

Mutations, 1998

Midnight Vultures, 1999

Chuck Berry

The Chess Box, 1988

The rock-and-roll poet set the standard

for all who would follow with classics like "Johnny B. Goode," "Maybellene," and "Rock and Roll Music," heard here in their original recorded form.

Big Brother and the Holding Company

Cheap Thrills, 1968

This album features Janis Joplin at her peak, moaning, screaming, and crying her way through "Summertime," "Piece of My Heart," and "Ball and Chain."

Bill Haley & His Comets

The Best of Bill Haley & His Comets, 1999

David Bowie

Ziggy Stardust and the Spiders from Mars, 1972

Bowie almost single-handedly invented glam and glitter rock. On this, his early seventies breakout album, he sings "Lady Stardust," "Soul Love," "Five Years," and other odes to a space alien.

Buddy Holly & The Crickets

The "Chirping" Crickets, 2004

The songs that put Buddy Holly on the top of the charts, and which were subsequently recorded by countless others in the years after his tragic death, are featured here.

The Doors

The Very Best of the Doors, 2001

This collection of number-one hits from Jim Morrison and the Doors provided the sound track to the counterculture revolution of the late 1960s and early 1970s.

Bob Dylan

Bringing It All Back Home, 1965

Dylan famously went electric on this album, which balances his raucous new sound on songs like "Subterranean Homesick Blues" and "Maggie Farm" with the poetic acoustic masterpieces "Gates of Eden" and "Mr. Tambourine Man."

Highway 61, 1965

Green Day

Nimrod, 1997

Warning, 2000

American Idiot, 2004

For its seventh album, Green Day wrote a rock opera about a character named Jesus of Suburbia, which sold more than 14 million copies. The internationally acclaimed album was turned into a stage play in 2009.

Jimi Hendrix

Are You Experienced?, 1967

Axis: Bold as Love, 1967

Hendrix produced only three studio albums—eight sides of vinyl—in just two years before his tragic death. This album not only shows Hendrix's wizardry on the guitar, but his mastery of electronic effects and recording techniques.

Electric Ladyland, 1968

Michael Jackson

Thriller, 1982

Jefferson Airplane

Surrealistic Pillow, 1967

Jefferson Airplane was the first group to sign with a major record label, and it is easy to see why with songs like "White Rabbit" and "Somebody to Love," which perfectly encapsulate the psychedelic sounds of San Francisco in 1967.

Led Zeppelin

Led Zeppelin, 1969

Led Zeppelin virtually invented heavy metal with this stunning debut album, which combined elements of blues, folk, and psychedelic rock into a sound many would imitate but few would master.

Led Zeppelin IV, 1971

Little Richard

Here's Little Richard, 1957

This is the first album from the man who claimed many times that he invented rock and roll. After listening to "Tutti Frutti," "Long Tall Sally," and "Rip It Up," it is hard to argue with that assertion.

Madonna

Like a Virgin, 1984

This album had American teens lining up outside record stores in much the same way their parents had done to buy Beatles' records.

Nirvana

Nevermind, 1991

The album that made Kurt Cobain an icon and celebrity, and likely led to his suicide, this collection of angry words and sludgy guitars features the grunge anthem "Smells Like Teen Spirit."

Pearl Jam

Ten, 1991

Pink Floyd

Dark Side of the Moon, 1973

One of the best-selling albums in history, *Dark Side of the Moon* is a sonic extravaganza about war and insanity that incorporates alarm clocks, wailing female backup vocals, and Dave Gilmour's soaring Stratocaster guitar.

Elvis Presley

Elv1s: 30 #1 Hits, 2002

This album, which also went straight to number one, is filled with Presley's finest, and it is not hard to see why he is called the King after hearing songs like "Heartbreak Hotel," "Hound Dog," and "Love Me Tender."

Prince

***Purple Rain*, 1984**

Red Hot Chili Peppers

***Blood Sugar Sex Magik*, 1991**

***Californication*, 1999**

R.E.M.

***Murmur*, 1983**

***Document*, 1987**

Featuring the hit "It's the End of the World As We Know It (And I Feel Fine)," this is the album that ignited the alternative rock explosion. In order to achieve a new sound and avoid sounding stale, the band's musicians swapped instruments in the studio and included new sounds like mandolins and saxophones.

Jimmie Rodgers

***The Very Best Of*, 2009**

The Rolling Stones

***Hot Rocks 1964–1971*, 1971**

This album contains the number-one songs that helped cement the Rolling Stones' reputation as one of the greatest rock bands in history.

Bruce Springsteen

***Born in the U.S.A.*, 1984**

Springsteen's dark commentary about the difficult state of life for working Americans in the 1980s is disguised here under radio-friendly pop melodies, synthesizers, and happy syncopation.

U2

***Unforgettable Fire*, 1984**

***The Joshua Tree*, 1987**

Lead singer Bono hung out with Bob Dylan, Van Morrison, and Keith Richards while writing this album, and incorporated blues and country into U2's cinematic sound on this Grammy-winning album.

Vampire Weekend

***Vampire Weekend*, 2008**

Vampire Weekend's eponymous album produced several popular singles with VW's trademark blend of sophisticated melodies, dance pop, and Afro pop. The song "Cape Cod Kwassa Kwassa" made it to *Rolling Stone*'s list of the 100 best songs of the year and got the band rewarded *Spin*'s best band of the year.

***Contra*, 2010**

Various Artists

***The Best of Jump & Jive*, 1999**

On this album, Louis Jordan, Wynonie Harris, Big Joe Turner, and many other artists lay down the foundations of rock and roll with jump blues, boogie-woogie, and swing music.

***Motown 1's*, 2004**

***Saturday Night Fever*, 1977**

***Woodstock*, 1994**

album: Originally used to describe a 12-inch (30cm) vinyl, long-playing (LP) record that played at 33 rpm (revolutions per minute) and could hold about twenty minutes of music on each side. In the digital age, an album is any collection of songs released together by an artist.

boogie-woogie: A fast-tempo, swinging or shuffling rhythm used in jazz, rock, and other pop music styles.

chord: A set of notes played simultaneously, as on a guitar or piano.

demographic: Part of a population, such as an age group, gender, or race.

gold: A term used for records that sell more than half a million copies.

hook: A memorable melody that catches, or hooks, the listener's attention.

platinum: A term used to describe records that sell more than a million copies. Multiplatinum records sell more than 2 million copies.

producer: In music, a producer works with a band to manage and oversee the recording process.

proto-punk: Music of the 1960s and early '70s that influenced the punk rock movement that began around 1975.

psychedelic: A word used to describe the hallucinatory effects of the drug LSD, from the Greek words meaning to manifest the soul or mind.

sample: Short segments of sounds from earlier recordings pasted together to form a new sound. Sampling is very popular with hip-hop and alternative rap artists.

single: Was originally used to refer to any record with a single song on each side. In the 1950s, singles were sold as 7-inch (17.7cm) vinyl records that played at 45 rpm (revolutions per minute). In the digital age, a single is any one song that is promoted separately from an album.

syncopation: A rhythmic style used in pop music in which the drummer highlights the second and fourth beats, or backbeats, in each four-beat measure.

synthesizer: An electronic instrument, usually played with a keyboard, that produces unique complex sounds or those that mimic other instruments such as violins and horns.

FOR MORE INFORMATION

Books

Jennifer Joline Anderson. *How to Analyze the Music of Michael Jackson*. Edina, MN: Abdo Publishing, 2011. This is an in-depth analysis of the musical techniques and styles Michael Jackson employed to become the King of Pop.

The Beatles. *The Beatles Anthology*. San Francisco: Chronicle Books, 2000. This four-hundred-page anthology contains rare photos and insightful text by the Beatles about the Beatles.

Brian J. Bowe. *The Ramones: American Punk Rock Band*. Berkeley Heights, NJ: Enslow Publishers, 2010. This book tells the story of the Ramones, from their blistering tempos to their stripped-down musical skills to their streetwise fashions that influenced a generation of punk rockers.

Marlene Targ Brill. *America in the 1970s*. Minneapolis: Lerner, 2009. The music of the 1970s was influenced by many aspects of the culture, and this book illuminates the disco era, with info about fashion, music, art, television, and movies.

Vincent Brunner. *Tunes: A Comic Book History of Rock and Roll*. New York: Universe, 2010. This unique book, written in a graphic novel format, covers rock-and-roll superheroes from Elvis Presley to the British Invasion and onward through the eras of punk, heavy metal, new wave, and grunge with wild and humorous illustrations.

Jim Corrigan. *The 1960s Decade in Photos: Love, Freedom, and Flower Power*. Berkeley Heights, NJ: Enslow Publishers, 2010. This book chronicles the events that influenced rock and roll in the 1960s using powerful photos of hippies, astronauts, and the Beatles.

Michele C. Hollow. *About the Grateful Dead: What a Long, Strange Trip It's Been*. Berkeley Heights, NJ: Enslow Publishers, 2009. This book serves as a history of the original jam band that kept the San Francisco sound alive from the 1960s until the death of lead guitarist Jerry Garcia in 1996.

Greg Prato. *Grunge is Dead*. Toronto: ECW Press, 2009. This book offers an oral history of the Seattle sound in the 1980s and '90s, as seen through the eyes and ears of those who witnessed the rise of Nirvana, Pearl Jam, and others.

Jeremy Roberts. *The Beatles: Music*

Revolutionaries. Minneapolis: Lerner, 2011. This is the story of one of the most commercially successful and critically acclaimed acts in the history of popular music, from their journey from Liverpool to the world stage and their work in genres ranging from folk rock to psychedelic pop.

Websites

AllMusic (www.allmusic.com) Originally known as All Music Guide (AMG), the AllMusic website is one of the most comprehensive music guides on the Internet. The site has in-depth information about old music, classics, and the latest hits, as well as descriptions of genres from opera to punk.

NME (New Musical Express) (www .nme.com) This is the online edition of the storied British music magazine, which has been publishing since 1952. The site provides music news, photos, video, blogs, reviews, and downloads with a British focus, but encompassing the latest sounds from the United States and elsewhere.

Pitchfork (www.pitchfork.com) Founded in 1995 and updated daily, Pitchfork focuses on criticism, commentary, and news concerning new music, especially underground and indie rock. The site is credited for breaking artists such as Arcade Fire and Modest Mouse.

Rolling Stone (www.rollingstone.com)

Rolling Stone has been covering pop stars and the music industry since the 1960s. The magazine's website contains the latest music and pop culture news, biographies of everyone from Jimmie Rodgers to Blink-182, and music, movie, and video reviews and downloads.

Films

A Hard Day's Night, 1964
This film introduced the charm and humor of the Beatles to a world audience, and spawned the concept of music videos.

Bullet in a Bible, 2005
This film documents the two biggest shows Green Day ever headlined, in which they played to more than one hundred thirty thousand people over the course of two days in the United Kingdom.

Don't Look Back, 1967
One of the first rock documentaries, this film covers Bob Dylan's 1965 tour of the United Kingdom as a solo artist with backstage antics, press conferences, and stunning performances.

The Filth and the Fury, 2000
This film covers the short career of the Sex Pistols and features elements of the social, political, and musical scene in Britain that helped launch the punk rock movement.

Hype, 1996
This documentary about the Seattle music scene features performances by Nirvana, Pearl Jam, and others,

and captures a moment in time when grunge exploded out of basements and garages into a pop culture phenomenon.

Monterey Pop, 1967

Filmed during the San Francisco hippie heyday, this concert movie features some of rock's top acts in their prime, including Janis Joplin, Jimi Hendrix, Otis Redding, the Mamas & the Papas, Jefferson Airplane, and the Who.

Saturday Night Fever, 1977

This drama about a young man drawn to a Manhattan discotheque popularized disco music across the globe. The sound track from the movie sold 15 million copies, stayed on the *Billboard* charts for 120 weeks, and remains the best-selling sound track of all time.

Stop Making Sense, 1984

Movie critic Leonard Maltin called this film, of the Talking Heads playing live in their funk punk prime, the greatest rock movie ever made.

This Is Spinal Tap, 1984

This "mockumentary" of the imaginary heavy metal band Spinal Tap satirizes the music and rock clichés put forth by bands of the new wave of British heavy metal.

Woodstock, 1969

This film popularized the counterculture Woodstock Nation by documenting stunning live performances by Santana, Janis Joplin, Jimi Hendrix, Crosby, Stills & Nash, and others while capturing the audience enjoying three days of peace, love, and music in upstate New York.

INDEX

PICTURE CREDITS

Cover: Alexandru Chiriac/Shutter stock.com

Andrew Whittuck/Redferns/Getty Images, 55

AP Images/Adam Rountree, 68

AP Images/Dan Grossi, 31

AP Images/Matthias Rietschel, 95

Charles Trainor/Time & Life Pictures/ Getty Images, 18

Ebet Roberts/Redferns/Getty Images, 73

Eugene Gologursky/WireImage/Getty Images, 105

Frank Micelotta/Getty Images, 83

Frank Mullen/WireImage/Getty Images, 70

© Jeff Albertson/Corbis, 64

Jeff Kravitz/FilmMagic/Getty Images, 99

John Franks/Keystone/Getty Images, 16

© Kevin P. Casey/Corbis, 100

© Kevin Fleming/Corbis, 12

KMazur/WireImage for Interscope Records/Getty Images, 88

Luciano Viti/Getty Images, 86

Michael Ochs Archives/Getty Images, 39

Michael Putland/Getty Images, 59, 75

© Minneapolis Star Tribune/ZUMA Press/Corbis, 34

© Neville Elder/Corbis, 108

Paul Warner/WireImage/Getty Images, 92

Peter Still/Redferns/Getty Images, 58

Petra Niemeier/Redferns/Getty Images, 25

© Photos 12/Alamy, 81

Richard E. Aaron/Redferns/Getty Images, 37

Robin Platzer/Time & Life Pictures/ Getty Images, 7

Ron Howard/Redferns/Getty Images, 42

Stuart A. Kallen, 48

Walter Iooss Jr./Getty Images, 51

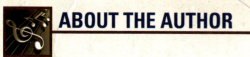

Stuart A. Kallen is the author of more than 250 nonfiction books for children and young adults. He has written extensively about science, the environment, music, culture, history, and folklore. In addition, Mr. Kallen has written award-winning children's videos and television scripts. In his spare time, he is a singer/songwriter/guitarist in San Diego, California.

DATE DUE